Praise for *People Buy f*

Beth Standlee is a true sales professional in all respects, and her writing embodies a delightful combination of humility and wit. With complete vulnerability, she artfully shares her unique perspectives on sales as demonstrated through her own life story. Whether you're considering a sales role, are new to the profession, or are an experienced sales veteran, *People Buy From People* is a fascinating must-read that delivers both encouragement and practical advice.

Brett A. Blair, executive coach and
Author of *From Autopilot to Authentic*

As a solopreneur, selling myself has always felt daunting. *People Buy From People* has changed that. While reading this book, I had so many "yes, me too!" moments because Beth Standlee connects with the reader through an outstanding combination of humility, personality, and straightforward expertise. It not only gave me confidence and a clear roadmap for personally selling myself and my business to others but also in handling day-to-day interactions with family and friends. This book is not just focused on sales techniques; it's about building confidence.

April Smith, owner, eContent Success

At a very young age I learned from my mom what the power of sales could do to shape someone's life and perspective. I was around six or seven years old when my mom took my sister and me shopping to spend our allowance money. The salesgirl only talked to my mom; she wouldn't give us smaller humans the time of day. I vividly remember my mom saying, "These girls are the important ones here. They have the money. Ask *them* what they're looking for."

That day, I learned that sales is about human connection—no matter how young or old you are. Whatever the circumstance, you're always selling something, whether you're deciding where to go for dinner, negotiating a new salary, or getting a kiddo to bed. The skills presented in this book will live with you for a lifetime. I can't wait for my mom to inspire your life the way she has mine.

Leslie Standlee
Proud daughter and sales executive

I've known Beth Standlee since 1998, and I've always been amazed that she finds it nearly impossible to see a negative situation when it comes to meeting a client's need. She oozes passion and enthusiasm. Beth has always recognized that meaningful conversations are the secret sauce to sales success.

I had the unique privilege of working alongside Beth in her firm for two years, and I learned more about selling in those two years than I had in the previous twenty. This book gives you great insight to Beth's sales and personal mind. You should take a peek!

Phil Showler
Director of sales at Amusement Products
and Pastor

I've known Beth Standlee for over twenty years, and I've never met a more compassionate person. Her love for people and her caring nature exude from her pores. *People Buy From People* comes from Beth's heart and tells the tale of how to not only be a success in sales, but a success in life. It's a must read for everyone!

Barbara Flynn
CEO, People First Inc.

People Buy From **People**

BETH STANDLEE

People Buy From People

How to Personally Connect in an Impersonal World

BETH STANDLEE

STONEBROOK
PUBLISHING

Stonebrook Publishing
Saint Louis, Missouri

A STONEBROOK PUBLISHING BOOK
Copyright © 2019 by Beth Standlee
This book was guided in development and
edited by Nancy L. Erickson, The Book Professor®
TheBookProfessor.com

Library of Congress Control Number: 2019935903

ISBN: 978-1-7322767-7-2

www.stonebrookpublishing.net

PRINTED IN THE UNITED STATES OF AMERICA

10 9 8 7 6 5 4 3 2 1

Dedication

This work is specifically dedicated to my husband, Jerry Standlee, who has kindly put up with anything I've ever wanted to do. His calm, matter-of-fact way of believing in me has made an unexplainable difference in my ability to always shoot for the stars. As a lifelong sales professional, I have a tendency to overexaggerate everything. Jerry's gentle way of helping me see things through—just as they are—has helped me finish many of the things I've started. Thank you, honey, for being sold on me and all the crazy ideas I've had through the years. I can't imagine what life would have been without you.

I also want to thank all those I hold so dear who really stuck with me as I trudged along for years, trying to get this book written. In my most insecure moments, my daughters Leslie and Amanda and my son Jordan, my closest friends Laura and Mary, my dear friend and bowling coach Susie, my mentor Nancy Starr, Joe and JaNelda Schumacker, the trusted group of CEOs in my CEO group, and Nancy Erickson, my book coach, never quit believing I could get the darn thing written. Thank you. I needed every listening ear, every word of encouragement, and every kick in the pants to see this project through to completion. I couldn't have done it without you.

Finally, I dedicate this book to you, the reader. I sincerely believe a career in sales can change your financial future and the freedom life holds for you. If you'll seriously latch on to the sales process laid out in this book and then temper that seriousness with a little fun, you'll experience the joy that comes from a professional career in sales. People love to buy stuff. Why not buy from you! I hope you enjoy the read, and please feel free to reach out to me.

I'd love to help.

Contents

Foreword

Someone once said that when Beth Standlee talks about sales, it goes from black and white to color. That's Beth. Her passion to help others never ends. Whether it's five people or five thousand, she has 'em in her hand. You can't say no to that passion. And she believes deeply that you can have it, too.

Beth has lived sales since the crib. In the ten years I've known her, I've watched as she has brought an audience of hundreds to tears. Her belief in the power of sales to change lives is profound.

And that's why Beth's book matters. Sales isn't arm-twisting manipulation or bludgeoning someone to buy something not needed. It's the inspired connection with another person to find a way to make life better.

Robert Louis Stevenson said everyone lives by selling something. For you, it may be a product, a service, Girl Scout cookies, your place in the organization, or a better idea of how to do things.

Yes, some people are born salespeople, and selling comes naturally to them. Yet the rest of us *can learn* the essentials, so we, too, can embrace the power of selling.

Beth knows the way and draws you along, telling you where each rock in the river is. She knows that sales is a science—a science that can be learned. And armed with the proper skills, you can make whatever you're selling come alive.

Passion in the presence of skill and wisdom leads to success and accomplishment.

If you believe that you're not selling something, don't stay there. Don't buy into what William James called "contempt prior to investigation." Think about it: You're selling something, even if *salesperson* isn't the title on your card.

An accountant sells the right way to look at money and numbers; a leader sells a way of doing things rather than dictating; a server sells the notion that a burger would be better with fries; a parent sells doing the right thing rather than what everybody else is doing.

Ask yourself, "What am I trying to make better with my work? What would it mean to me if I were better at that 'sale'? What misery could I diminish if I were better at communicating the value of my work?"

I first heard Peter Drucker quote Robert Louis Stevenson when I was with Vistage, the CEO organization. Gradually, a life-changing realization came upon me. Acknowledging that everyone lives by selling something was the key to how people behave in organizations. I went from being a terrified manager who thought I had to know all the answers to a passionate, inspired leader who painted the possible. Never again would I find it necessary to dictate. I learned to sell. And I began to understand what others were selling.

Had I known Beth back then, I would have saved a lot of precious time.

Experience Beth's book. Find the skills to match your desires, and you'll inspire your mission.

Nancy Starr
CEO Leadership Coach
and Mentor to the Stars

1

How Can Being a Sales Professional Change Your Life?

t's an interesting question: How can being a sales professional change your life? It's also a highly relevant question as people are searching for a way to *be* more, *have* more, *live* more, *feel* more, and *find* a better future. That's why it was so important for me to write this story. A career in sales changed my life.

I believe if people—women in particular—come to understand that a career in sales can give them more financial and personal freedom, their lives will be better, fuller.

Before I get into the strategies that made me successful, I want to share my own "better life" story with you.

I'm pretty sure we're not so different from each other. I ran the gamut of early childhood

> I believe if people—women in particular—come to understand that a career in sales can give them more financial and personal freedom, their lives will be better, fuller.

sales with lemonade stands and Girl Scout cookies. Because of the natural competitor in me, I wasn't afraid to ask people to buy things. That's a real advantage for a cute little girl selling cookies or being the lemonade czar of the neighborhood! However, once puberty hit and self-doubt showed up with the onset of all those hormones, the idea of selling anything gave way to braces and pimples.

After I graduated in 1979 from Northside High in Fort Smith, Arkansas, I traveled down the road to Conway to pursue a degree at the University of Central Arkansas. Eventually, I hoped to go to law school. Instead, at the tender age of eighteen, I met the love of my life during the second semester of my freshman year.

Pining for Jerry, who had graduated that spring and moved to Kansas City, I took a summer job selling Southwestern Books. As part of the training, I spent a week in Nashville learning everything I could about selling books door-to-door. The training was spectacular. Each day the indoctrination started at 7:59 a.m. and ended at 9:59 p.m., which was the same schedule they wanted us to keep when we spent our summer in the field selling books. At the end of that week, I received my assignment and moved to Bristol, West Virginia.

I was convinced I'd be the superstar of the summer. I thought the long hours of work would help me not miss Jerry so much. Plus, I was going to make more than ten thousand dollars in twelve short weeks. That was a lot of money for a college student in 1980.

I told my parents and my boyfriend, "No matter what, I'm spending the summer selling these books door-to-door. Even if I call and want to come home, please encourage me to stay here and sell these books."

I had big goals and was successful every day I was in the field—which turned out to be exactly four. Instead of being caught up in the drive to sell the most books, I was miserable—not with the sales part of the job; that was pretty easy. They had trained us well, and the product was good. No, the problem was priorities.

I was only nineteen years old. I was on the tennis team at school and needed to practice during the summer. I missed Jerry. And I'm pretty sure I didn't really want to work six days a week from 7:59 a.m. to 9:59 p.m.

So on day four, I called my dad at work, something I'd never done before. He was a butcher, and I'm not even sure how they called him off the floor to get him on the phone. He listened. I could hear the concern in his voice as he said, "Go make one more sales call and then call me back."

I made that next sales call and sold a set of books. With check in hand, I found the nearest pay phone and called my dad again. He congratulated me on the sale and asked if I felt better. Crying, I told him that I didn't feel a bit better.

"Well, baby," he said, "you made this commitment, and I encourage you to stay out there this summer and meet the goals you set for yourself."

Since calling my dad hadn't worked, I phoned Jerry. He's a wonderful listener and always has been. He's the kind of person who allows other people to make up their own mind. But he gave me the same advice as Dad: go out and make one more sales call. So I went to the next house and sold another set of books. The universe was trying to show me that I could make it. I just didn't want to listen.

I called Jerry back with another check in hand. He couldn't handle my tears. He offered to come to West Virginia to bring me home.

I couldn't do that. There was a prescribed way we were supposed to leave the field. I'd have to go back to Nashville and check out before I could leave. I needed to turn in my orders and my sales case, and I couldn't bear to think of how bad all this was going to look. I'd been the favorite student during training. I was voted most likely to succeed. The number of kids who stayed out all summer was incredibly low, and I didn't want to be one of the ones who failed. And I couldn't stop crying.

At this point, Jerry was at a loss. After a bit of silence, my sweet boyfriend cleared his throat and said, "Tell them you're getting married."

I didn't say a word. I'm pretty sure I stopped breathing completely. I definitely wanted to marry this man, but I couldn't tell if he was proposing or simply offering a good excuse for me to come home. The seconds seemed like minutes. Then he said, "We don't really have to get married. I'll meet you in Nashville and you can come home." I packed my stuff right away and drove straight to Nashville.

To be clear, I really enjoyed selling those books. The delight on the families' faces was priceless, but the amount of work it required was something I was unable to manage. Hindsight is 20/20. Almost forty years later, I can see how I could have balanced that summer and enjoyed a different kind of success, but I have no regrets. The sales training I received was something no one can ever take from me, and it became a foundation that's served me well.

> The sales training I received was something no one can ever take from me, and it became a foundation that's served me well.

I returned to Conway in July and signed up for my sophomore year back at the University of Central Arkansas. Jerry and I saw each another a couple of times over the summer and talked about getting married after I finished my sophomore year. For his birthday in August, several of our friends and I went to Kansas City to see him and some other friends who lived there. Soon after that trip, we changed our plans from getting married in May to having a baby in May. I was pregnant.

I didn't know I was with child right away. It wasn't until two weeks into the semester that my pregnancy was confirmed. The conversations in my head were relentless. *Now everyone knows I'm not smart enough to use protection. I'm an unwed teenage mother.*

How could I be so stupid? I am NOT having an abortion. I love Jerry. What if he doesn't really love me? and on and on and on.

Since we didn't live in the same town, Jerry and I talked about our options over the phone. I'm pretty stubborn, and I let him know I could do this baby thing on my own. I loved this man more than I can articulate here, but I did *not* want him to marry me because he thought he had to. In his calm way, he decided to call my dad to ask for my hand in marriage.

It seemed like a lifetime before Jerry called me back. In truth, it was probably only fifteen minutes or so. He's a man of few words and gets to the point rather quickly.

When my phone rang, I answered right away.

"How'd it go?" I asked.

"I asked your dad if I could marry you."

"What did he say?"

"He asked me if I loved you."

"And…"

"Well, I said yes."

"And then?"

"Your dad said okay."

"What did mom say?"

"Your mom said, 'Is she pregnant?'"

"Oh my GOD! What did you say?"

"Yes."

And that's how I closed the biggest deal of my life. I laughingly say that I got my MRS. during my sophomore year of college and my MOM shortly thereafter.

But as a teen bride and a very young mother with no degree, I worried about what people thought of me. As a matter of fact, when I met with the dean of admissions to withdraw from school, I had one of the most awkward encounters of my life. With all the self-judging conversations swirling in my head, I couldn't believe it when he looked across the desk during my exit interview and asked, "How far along are you?" I was shocked! How could he possibly know I was pregnant?

My face burned with embarrassment and shame as I looked up and said, "Oh, just about six or seven weeks."

Then a weird thing happened. He blushed and said awkwardly, "Congratulations. However, I was referring to your student status. Are you a freshman, sophomore…?"

I nearly died! Honestly, sinking into the floor and disappearing would have been better than finishing that conversation.

I didn't die, but I wound up needing a lot of affirmation that everything was going to be okay—that I was going to be okay. The reality was, I felt "less than." I had not followed my plan. I was not going to college to eventually become a lawyer. Now my new plan was to figure out how to be a wife and mom.

Jerry and I moved to San Antonio, Texas, where Leslie was born. After a year away from school, I walked on and received a scholarship to play tennis for the University of Texas at San Antonio. I was definitely a nontraditional student athlete.

That lasted two years because at Christmas break, I found out I was pregnant with Amanda.

Jerry was hired by the FAA when all the air traffic controllers went on strike during the Reagan era, which moved us from San Antonio to Oklahoma City, where Amanda was born, then on to Houston, and finally to Amarillo.

Once again, any plan that I had seemed undone or in need of a redo. Don't get me wrong, I loved my wonderful husband and my two beautiful daughters. But something wasn't working inside. I felt like I needed to do more or be more. Maybe I thought it wasn't enough to be my children's mother, my husband's wife, or my parents' daughter. Perhaps it's a generational thing. I hope so. I'm not proud of the fact I felt this way.

Nonetheless, this is where I was when I met Mary Lou Benson, a Tupperware manager in Amarillo, Texas.

Mary Lou was amazing. She had the kind of light in her eyes that made her look like she was smiling all the time. When she picked me up in her Tupperware Oldsmobile station wagon and explained that I could have one just like hers when I recruited five other people to sell Tupperware, I got pretty excited. As a young mom of two little girls whose husband worked a different shift every day—and even that changed weekly—having a second car sounded glorious! And Tupperware would even pay the insurance. That was July of 1984; by December we were a two-car family.

I earned nine brand-new vehicles during my tenure at Tupperware. Each time I earned a new car, my confidence grew. I don't know exactly what happened in me, but somehow the outward symbol of success helped me be even more proud of being my children's mom and my husband's wife. I learned a lot about selling during the eleven years I spent with Tupperware. I studied at the feet of greats like Zig Ziglar, Norman Vincent Peale, Og Mandino, and Tony Robbins.

From a personal point of view, I know I'm more confident today than I was then, and selling helped a lot! I learned that my husband wasn't in charge of making my day great. I couldn't sit at home waiting for him to entertain me. I was responsible for my own life.

I've learned to accept myself in a way that doesn't require affirmation from others. Don't get me wrong, I still have that kind of people-pleasing personality that seeks outside approval. It's something I work on daily. In a way, I think that's why being in sales works so well for me. When someone buys something from me, there's that immediate feedback of knowing that I got it right. I sincerely believe I've helped someone.

I've never sold anything that didn't make a difference in the buyer's life. I learned early on from Zig Ziglar that "you can

I've never sold anything that didn't make a difference in the buyer's life.

have everything in life you want, if you will just help other people get what they want."

I'm a lot more comfortable in my own skin today. I'm not nearly as attached to the belief that I can actually control the outcome, which leaves a ton of room for everything and everyone. It helps in sales *and* in my life! Today I'm confident. I'm okay (most of the time) if people don't like me or don't buy from me or don't call me back.

But there's one thing I don't like. I don't like it when people tell me no. The distaste for hearing no is something I figured out early in my sales career, and it still serves me well today. Even though I don't like it when someone tells me no, I'm no longer linked to the negativity of that no. I can step back and say to myself, "They said no to buying my stuff, not no to me." There's a difference—an important difference.

My life is better because I'm a sales professional. I found my way as a parent, a wife, and a saleswoman because I created a new sense of worth that works for me. The anxiety of my younger years has vanished.

Everything was hard in the beginning, and I used to cry when I couldn't get the deal. It was devastating. I would play the scene over and over and over in my mind, wondering where I went wrong. YUCK! Such a waste of emotion when I could have spent that time and energy creating the next opportunity—or finding the next thing I wanted to sell.

After some great successes, I moved on from Tupperware and sold cars for a while. Ninety days to be exact. I thought it was fun to help someone get a new car, and I sold thirty vehicles during those ninety days. However, many of those buyers felt

I was trying to get one over on them, so they'd come in ready for a fight. That wasn't my idea of helping someone.

So I moved on to selling group and party events in the family entertainment industry. It was definitely an extension of what I'd learned holding Tupperware parties for more than a decade. Event sales were great. I worked with companies, fundraising organizations, schools, birthday parties, and more. All along, I learned more and more about sales. Eventually, I decided I wasn't making enough money and began looking at other sales opportunities.

At this point, my sales career took an interesting leap. I responded to an ad and interviewed for a sales job at a software company in Dallas. It seemed like a good fit. They were looking for someone with more than five years of sales experience, so I figured that with my fifteen-plus years of selling, I'd be the perfect candidate.

But when the interviewer realized I hadn't finished my college degree, he ended the interview abruptly. It didn't matter that I had almost two decades of sales experience and three years of college under my belt.

Honestly, I was pretty devastated. However, I gathered the courage to go back to school and wound up selling software and hardware for the amusement industry!

I guess, on the one hand, I ought to thank that guy. That's the kind of situation that winds up being a catalyst for change. I'm pretty sure I would have gone back to school, regardless. Every year I kept thinking I would, but until that gut-punching interview occurred, I never took action.

It's funny. I remember someone asking me at graduation what I was going to do now that I had my degree. My response was, "I'm going to keep selling. It is the way I make my living." I have to admit though, it is nice to have the degree.

I was forty-two when I walked across the stage in my cap and gown. It was a very cool weekend at my house because we'd driven to Texas A&M the previous day to celebrate my older daughter, Leslie's, graduation. We had a big party at the house. All my friends came at 7:00 p.m. and as the old crowd was leaving at 9:30 p.m., Leslie's young grads showed up to party! That's when I began to really see myself as a sales professional. The degree didn't change the experience I'd gained throughout the years, but when I actually graduated, there was something in my head and my heart that was a little different. I must have needed outside confirmation of the diploma backing up what I already had on the inside. It's probably silly that a piece of paper helped, but I think it did.

Today, that degree hangs on my wall. It is a symbol of completion and a necessary piece of paper that opens the door for some opportunities. However, I believe as you make your way through this book, you can be in a position to create a professional sales career for yourself with or without a degree.

The process for selling is so simple. The difficulty can come with the discipline and commitment to practice and follow the process consistently. My promise to you is that by the end of this book, you'll be convinced that there's a way for you to celebrate the personal and financial freedom that comes with a career in professional sales.

Two and half years after I earned my diploma, I quit my six-figure software sales job and started a coaching and training company, TrainerTainment®, which serves the hospitality industry. I discovered people were buying capital equipment from me because I went onsite and trained them how to use our product to sell more events for their entertainment centers. In *The E-Myth Revisited*, Michael E. Gerber says that people who start their own companies have an "entrepreneurial seizure" and decide, "I can do better!"

Learning that I could teach others to sell well made a big difference. That deep desire to help others is, and always has been, a driving force in my sales career and my life. I believe there is a uniqueness about women that gives us an edge when it comes to helping others. We have an innate quality of service. I'm not saying that men don't also have this terrific ability. What I'm saying is that women may be built in such a way that it's their superpower.

What I've learned in my life is that sales professionals must recognize that they have the ability to cultivate, create, and connect with ideal relationships. When you couple that ability with a realization that you've come to a point in your life where you're willing to buck the system and ask for what you want or need, then you might be poised to take that leap into a new career.

Take it from me. A professional sales career can change your life. The freedom of knowing that your time and finances are directly linked to how many calls you're willing to make gives you a sense of empowerment that affects not only your professional life, but your personal world as well. So if you have a sincere belief that *great selling is about helping others,* I encourage you to keep reading and find out how you can excel.

2

Something's Holding Me Back. What Is It?

I f you think something's holding you back from pursuing a fun and fulfilling sales career, you're probably right! At least that's been my experience. Over the years, I've learned that it's my own *limiting beliefs* that create situations that hold me back. I'm sure you're familiar with the saying, "It's all in your head." Well, I think that might be exactly right.

If you want to change your behavior, you first have to change what you believe. With that in mind, let's look at how *eliminating your limiting beliefs* is the first step to enjoying the personal and financial freedom that a sales profession offers you.

Limiting Beliefs

To have a limiting belief means to *restrict* or *confine* an opinion or conviction about something. For me, this shows up in the vision I have of myself, of my work, of others, or about situations that suggest I can't do something. But when you face up to your limiting beliefs, you can right-size them and stop creating the mental catastrophes that prevent you from becoming a successful sales professional.

There've been many times when I felt that I couldn't pick up the phone to make a single call. I was too depressed. I didn't think anyone wanted to talk to me. I felt I wasn't good enough. I couldn't bear rejection. Every one of those thoughts represents a limiting belief and was certain to create a negative outcome for that sales day.

Other limiting beliefs I've had fall in the category of "I don't have enough," such as I don't have enough knowledge, or leads, or education; or the right personality; or the right boss. I think these types of beliefs are pretty common, and they may match your own long list!

A common belief that could hold you back from a sales career is that you might think salespeople are *smarmy*. Perhaps you picture that uncle who shows up for Thanksgiving dressed in his plaid used-car salesman jacket, snaps his fingers, and says, "Hey, have I got a deal for you!" The difference between this guy and the sales professional is profound. A real sales professional believes way down deep inside that they truly make a difference in the world. I can tell you that I've never sold anything that I didn't believe would help the buyer.

I'm a persuasive, enthusiastic person, and it can be easy for me to talk people into wanting the things I want them to have. But I don't do that. I have a process I follow to determine if what I have to offer matches what they need and/or want. When all that lines up, great! I'll sell them something they're very lucky to have. No tricks. Nothing smarmy.

Slick selling techniques don't work anymore. So you can ditch your poor opinion of salespeople. The used-car salesman of old doesn't get very far in today's selling environment.

How do you get rid of your limiting beliefs—the not-enoughs and the inaccurate perceptions? It won't be by rah-rah and cheering yourself on to victory. That usually doesn't work for me, although I'm an affirmation type of gal and I do pray a lot. I have, however, found a three-step process that helps me spring into action more quickly and pulls me out of the muck of my own limiting beliefs.

Step 1: Notice the Belief

Recognize it. Name it. Call it out. Acknowledge it exists. Do what Zig Ziglar recommends: "Discuss a fear and it disappears!" Here's how that might look:

Sample Belief: *No one wants to talk to me.* When you say something out loud, you can begin to call it into question. Martin E.P. Seligman wrote a wonderful book called *Learned Optimism: How to Change Your Mind and Your Life.* If you're locked into your own limiting beliefs, Seligman's book is a must-read. It ignites the conversion of those beliefs into something that works *for* you rather than *against* you. There's something magical about getting the negative thoughts out of your head. You can acknowledge them in the open. Often, when you articulate those beliefs, they don't sound as daunting.

Step 2: Get Curious

Ask yourself *why* you think no one wants to talk to you. You may answer in that all-or-nothing way and say, "No one ever picks up their phone." Is that true all the time? I bet not.

A better question comes from my friend and mentor, Nancy Starr, who asks me over and over again when I'm stuck in my own limiting beliefs, "What else could be true?" Every time I give her an answer, she keeps drilling down, and sometimes she asks me this question four or five times in a row. By the end of the session, I've usually forgotten what the limiting belief was.

When you limit your belief about what's possible, it's too easy to stay stuck in a paralyzed state. *Stuck* is a tough place to be. I picture being in quicksand up to my knees.

Curiosity is better. When you're curious, you'll more easily find the secret recipe to move forward. If you examine the belief that "no one wants to talk to me" or "they never pick up their phone," you might realize that the phone isn't a good way to connect that day. So you ask, "What else could be true?"

and discover that going to see someone in person is another option. When you ask the question again, you may decide to send a follow-up email. And then you get even more creative and check in through social media to see if you can catch the prospect's attention.

Curiosity leads to action, and the right kind of action can create results. Action moves you away from being stuck.

Step 3: Be Reasonable

Examine whether that belief is something you would lay on someone else. Here's what I mean. Let's say you keep working on your list of prospects, but you never actually call any of them. I've seen salespeople work for weeks to get a good list of names together. Their limiting belief in this situation is, "I don't know who to call on first. I have to get the list right before I can make that call."

If you were coaching someone, how would you react to this limiting belief, to their paralysis? My guess is you'd tell them to pick up the phone and call the first person on the list! You'd encourage them to *do something,* to take action. Getting started may be the hardest step, but it's essential.

Education and mastery build confidence. Confidence erodes limiting beliefs. Limiting beliefs are usually rooted in fear and what-ifs that aren't true now and will never be.

The benefit of calling into question your own limiting beliefs is that you can face the fears and facts that are holding you back. The negative beliefs lose their control when you have a system that says, "Wait a minute ... What's *really* going on here? Is this true *all* the time?" When limiting beliefs control us, we tend to catastrophize things—just like if you have a fender-bender, and your mind immediately jumps to, "I totaled my car," when you actually only bumped the guy in front of you.

If you want a very clear system to question your beliefs in a quick and beautiful way, check out Byron Katie's book, *Loving*

What Is: Four Questions That Can Change Your Life. I don't know anyone who's more committed to helping people live more fully by eliminating the thoughts that hold them back.

I encourage you to take action *now*. List all the beliefs you hang on to, the ones that you know hold you back. No one else is going to read your list, so be thorough. Make the list, acknowledge the belief, write down why you think the belief is there, and then get very curious about that belief. I encourage you to ask yourself the question, "What else could be true?" at least three times for each limiting belief.

My friend Mary has the limiting belief that she's not a salesperson. That's not unusual; most people don't think they're sales-oriented. But the truth is that we're all trying to get someone to buy or buy off on our idea, service, product, friendship. We do it all the time.

Mary was one of my very best Tupperware hostesses back in the day, which meant that she held many Tupperware parties in her home. She was quite adamant that she wasn't a salesperson—and she still holds to that claim today—however, I sold more plastic bowls at Mary's parties than with any other hostess I ever had. She would never take credit for the fact that she "sold" all those people on coming to her house for a party.

Mary attended Tupperware recruiting rallies with me and was recognized as the hostess with the mostess! There was always a time at those rallies when we tempted those great hostesses to become dealers so they could actually make money selling Tupperware. You guessed it: My "non-sales" friend, Mary, joined Tupperware.

She would never admit that she was or is good at sales, but she got really good at a lot of things she didn't know she could do before she spread her wings a bit. I've pulled Mary through a lot of her own limiting beliefs during our friendship.

Mary is now the director of operations in my company. She took her first college class when she was thirty-nine years old and got her degree in short order, so she could help the most troubled fifth-graders in her school have a better life. She recently purchased a hundred-year-old home in Comfort, Texas, and operates this majestic place as a wonderful bed and breakfast. No sales needed there, right?

Mary is very black and white in her thinking, and sometimes, like all of us, she allows her limiting beliefs to get in the way. What I admire about Mary is that she has a certain way of paying attention. She's curious about how things might be. She's not close-minded, and she's never been a know-it-all. Mary understands that the limits she places on herself hold her back.

Luckily, she has me—the Lucy to her Ethel—to help her see when she's limited her thinking. (For the record, I'm not sure she thinks it's lucky, but I'm pretty sure she loves me anyway!)

So when you find yourself in a spot where you're stuck and your negative thoughts are getting in the way, I encourage you to ask: "What else could be true? What more could there be for me, for the people I serve, for my family if I set this belief aside for this minute?" If that doesn't work, find a friend who will push you into the deep end of the pool from time to time.

Adopt a Client-Centered Sales Approach

When you get past the fear of taking the first step to pick up the phone and call a potential customer, you want to have a positive experience. You need a successful process to reinforce the new belief of "I want to improve my financial and personal freedom with a career in sales."

One thing that's worked well for me is to follow a *client-centered sales approach*. This approach has made a big difference in my comfort level and in my success.

If you're in sales, when you ask people for their hard-earned dollars, it can be uncomfortable, depending on your relationship and beliefs around money. The funny thing is, when you get the sales process right, the money thing is easy. (By the way, here's a big news flash: buyers know you want their money!)

The strength of having a sales process is that it creates *competence*, and competence breeds *confidence*. Having confidence can eliminate the limiting beliefs that come from the fear of not knowing what or why you need to do what you need to do. So let me give you a peek at the sales process we will work on more as we get deeper into this book.

> The strength of having a sales process is that it creates *competence, and competence breeds confidence.*

The PCQPC Sales Method—The Only Sales Process You'll Ever Need!

It's a bold promise, but it will ring true when you have the discipline to implement it every time you're in a selling situation. Whether you're calling on a client for the first time or in the final closing stages of the deal, you'll want to make sure you use each step of the sales process.

Every successful person has a strategy or a proven process that helps get them through the day. The coach of a winning football team relies on the playbook. An award-winning chef creates recipes that are irresistible. It only makes sense that a sales professional who uses the discipline of a tried and true sales process can compete at the top of their field.

We're going to dig into every step of this proven system throughout the book, but here's a sneak peek at how the PCQPC sales process works:

Prospect, Connect, Qualify, Propose, and Close

- **Prospect:** Find and target your ideal buyer. (chapter 5)

- **Connect:** Create comfort and trust. Begin to build the relationship. (chapter 6)

   As we dive deep into the sales process, you'll learn that connection in and of itself isn't the thing that will make you a great salesperson. Rather, I believe connection is the *first step* in a multitiered sales process. Learning to do it well can make all the difference in your success.

   For me, the big learning came when I realized that people wouldn't necessarily buy from me just because they liked me. There is a lot more to the sales process than being able to connect with the right kind of buyer. In the following chapters, we'll look closely at how to strengthen the connection part of the process and use that strength as the foundation for creating lasting relationships that in turn create lifetime customers. When you connect well with others, a deep sense of trust and comfort appear.

- **Qualify:** Understand what the buyer wants so you can sell them that. (chapter 7)

   I've always said, "Find out what the customer wants and then sell them that!" It seems too simple, but it works. Once I figured out that it was *not* about me or my product, I got really curious about the buyer. What makes them tick? What is it about them that would make my product or service irresistible? I can't know these things if I don't get super curious about what's going on with the buyer. If I could reshape each sales person's brain so they feel more like a journalist or a private detective than a sales rep, then it might be easier to teach the qualification part of the sales process.

   Full disclosure: qualification is my favorite part of the sales process. It's so much easier to be interested in the buyer than to try to work interesting information about my product into the conversation. There are five specific things you need to know about the buyer's situation before you start presenting a solution. Once you know these five things, you'll always be in a better position to present the best solution to your potential customer. I promise, you'll close more often and sooner than you have in the past!

- **Propose:** Present a solution that adds total value to what the buyer wants and needs. (chapter 8)

   The most important thing to remember is that you want to be in constant conversation with the buyer.

Often, once we start talking about our products or service, it can be so easy to switch the dialogue into a monologue. And you don't want to do that.

People always say you have to be sold on your own product in order to sell it to others. In fact, you must be sold on what your product *can do* for others and focus during your proposal on the buyer's needs as they relate to your product. Our products often have features and benefits that mean a lot to us as sellers, and we feel obligated to share all that information—like sharing all the details adds value. But I've found that great proposals include *only* the features and benefits that match the desires of the buyer. If not, you're wasting your air and the buyer's time. And worse, you may confuse the buyer or complicate the sale altogether.

Present your product based on what you learned during the qualify step. Tie back each relevant product feature or benefit based on what you learned during the first two steps of the sales process.

- **Close:** Ask for the order. (chapter 9)

  Closing the sale may seem like the most important part of the sales process. But I've found that when you get the other steps right, closing becomes the quickest step. That may sound odd but, honestly, every step prior to asking for the order is a setup for this part of the process. Of course, you can't simply wait for the fish to jump in the boat. You have to make a request of the buyer. I call this the "next step" moment.

  Classically, people refer to the close as the moment when you get the deposit, a signature on the agreement, or some type of financial transaction takes place. But I think every sales encounter has some type of close or next step. Other nonfinancial closing moments are:

- Setting up the next appointment with a time and date, not something vague like, "I'll call you next week."

- Learning who the decision maker is and scheduling the next meeting with him or her.

- Getting a proposal together and scheduling the proposal review with the decision maker.

- Even when someone tells me to "buzz off," it's a closing moment. I know what to do with the potential client. I mark them off my list and move on to someone else.

All the work happens in the first three steps of the sales process. Closing the sale is a direct result of understanding what the buyer wants/needs, offering a solution that makes sense, and asking for the money.

Now that you understand the internal stuff that could be holding you back, let's move on to all those external things that can get in the way of your success.

3

How to Stack the Deck in Your Favor

gainst all odds—teenage bride, young mom, no degree—I figured out how to play the proverbial hand that was dealt to me. However, during my sales career, and especially during my sales coaching tenure, there were plenty of times that an adjustment in attitude and change of behavior was critical for me to be successful.

Don't get me wrong. When sales are plentiful, life looks very good. However, when times get tough, the I-can-do-no-wrong conversations turn into anxiety-filled thoughts of, "I'm not good enough to do this job." I'm certain that I'm not the only salesperson who's faced this type of self-doubt.

I once worked with a new salesperson in Kansas City, Missouri. Lisa had everything you could want in a sales rep. She was young, energetic, and smart. Although she didn't have much experience in professional sales, her desire for success seemed to outweigh her lack of sales know-how.

As I began the coaching process with her, we cultivated lead lists and focused on target markets. She worked with people inside the business to learn our product. She practiced and mastered the sales process until she was finally ready to talk with prospective buyers. Lisa's enthusiasm was contagious.

She seemed ready to grow the new business that our company desperately needed.

That's when the challenges began. First, Lisa was unhappy with her business cards. The phone number for the office was printed on her cards, but she wanted to have her cell number listed instead. So she waited to make any sales calls until her business cards were reprinted. Next, she wasn't confident that she knew the product well enough. She thought she needed more training. Unbelievably, when her new business cards came in, she expressed frustration over the leave-behind marketing materials. She didn't think the brochure did a good enough job of "selling" the product.

You can imagine that, as her coach, I was pretty frustrated that Lisa wouldn't get out the door to make a single sales call. Our company had worked hard to be sure that our new salespeople had everything they needed. I felt like her issue was much bigger than needing a perfect brochure, fancy business cards, or more training. At some point, whether you're a salesperson, doctor, lawyer, or burger flipper, you have to take the initiative and do the job. Nike has it right with their "Just Do It" slogan.

It's probably no surprise that Lisa didn't last long. I think she was scared, which is pretty normal in sales. Nevertheless, a good salesperson finds a way to move forward. Lisa was at a standstill. She continued to spout excuses about why she wasn't ready to go into the field. Maybe she thought that buyers would magically fall at her feet if only she had the right stuff to present to them. Perhaps she imagined that she could hand out a beautiful brochure and her business card, and the dollars would fall from heaven. Or, conversely, that if she didn't have these things, she couldn't make a sale. At any rate, she kept insisting that she needed more, more, more, in order to succeed.

Sales is fun, and it can be easy. But there's no magic. You have to do the work. Sales is about asking for what you want on every level, whether inside the company or with the buyer. The truth is that you rarely need anything more than yourself, the buyer, and a great product or service that meets a need.

> **The truth is that you rarely need anything more than yourself, the buyer, and a great product or service that meets a need.**

From a coaching point of view, Lisa taught me a lot. I realized that when it comes to being a great sales professional, there are many excuses (real or imagined) that can prevent you from getting out the door. So I came up with a formula that would help my next sales student understand that we had the right cards to play, no matter the game.

Here are six key behaviors that will help you stack the deck in your favor so you can play a winning hand:

1. Take ownership of your training.

Know Yourself

You're the only one who can determine how much you need to know to have the confidence to get out and sell. It's important to understand yourself and your style, and to do that, I recommend you check into Kolbe, at kolbe.com. The Kolbe A assessment measures the conative part of your brain, which is an indicator of how you instinctively take action.

One parameter that Kolbe measures is how a person handles information. They call this assessment category the "fact finder." My experience is the higher the fact-finding score, the more information a person needs in order to thrive in their role. My fact-finding score is a four out of ten. While I need the pertinent information, I don't always need *all* the information. As a matter of fact, I'd rather have the *Reader's Digest* condensed version of just about everything.

Another assessment category is the "quick start" indicator, which measures the level of risk a person is willing to take, as well as how quickly they may jump into action. My quick-start number is very high, which means I want to get going as soon as possible. If you consider that my low fact-finding score is coupled with a high quick-start number, you'll realize that I'm a sales rep who wants to get out the door as soon as I have enough information to make the first call.

I suspect that Lisa had a high, rather than low, fact-finding number. I wish I'd known about the Kolbe assessment tool at the time. It would have helped me to be more patient, and I would have valued the fact that she really did need a lot more information than I'd given her.

Read Books

I've learned a lot from reading what other great sales pros have written. Jim Rohn said, "You gotta read!" He was right. Reading is critical for salespeople.

I don't put everything I read into practice, but I do filter what I think might work for me and give those things a try. Some of my favorite sales gurus are:

- Zig Ziglar, *See You at The Top: The "How To" book that gives YOU a "Check Up" from the "Neck Up" to Eliminate "Stinkin Thinkin" and AVOID "Hardening of the Attitudes"*

- Duane Sparks, *The New Action Selling: How to Sell Like a Professional Even If You Think You Are One*

- Jeffrey Gitomer, *The Little Red Book of Selling: 12.5 Principles of Sales Greatness*

- Og Mandino, *The Greatest Salesman in the World: You Can Change Your Life With The Wisdom Of Ten Ancient Scrolls Handed Down For Thousands Of Years*

- Mike Weinberg, *New Sales Simplified: The Essential Handbook for Prospecting and New Business Development*

- Mark Hunter, *High-Profit Prospecting: Powerful Strategies to Find the Best Leads and Drive Breakthrough Sales Results*

- Jill Konrath, *SNAP Selling: Speed Up Sales and Win More Business with Today's Frazzled Customers*

- Daniel H. Pink, *To Sell Is Human: The Surprising Truth About Moving Others*

I could offer more authors, but this list is a good start. And, of course, you're reading this book, which I believe is also a must-read for sales professionals.

Practice What You Learn

Here's what happens to me during training or when I read: I discover things I want to try out. I "load my lips," so to speak. I practice my pitch. A lot of times when I practice, I feel as if my lips won't work, so I try again. Training is about showing up for practice and running a play over and over again. You can't build a muscle if you don't use it.

I rehearse what I might say to a prospective buyer in my head. Then I practice it out loud with my husband or with a friend or co-worker; and then—eventually—I try it out on the customer. Sometimes things come out smoothly and sometimes I sound like a goofball. Either way, I learn.

My point is that training and practice are both necessary. Eventually, you have to try out the new techniques you're learning. In order to grow, you must take a leap of faith and try something new—even if you're afraid you're not quite ready.

We had a salesperson at TrainerTainment who'd completed all the training I thought she needed, but she was still struggling to get out the door. I asked her a question.

"What do you need now to be confident enough to talk to a potential customer?"

"I need to know they'll buy, and I need the experience of closing the sale," she answered.

That was a real head-scratcher for me. I thought she'd had enough training and was competent enough to make the sales call. But if she needed to be certain the prospect would buy *and* she needed the experience of closing a sale in order to be confident, I didn't how she'd ever reach out to a prospect. Experience builds confidence, so you have to take your training and put it into practice—over and over again. You build confidence by doing.

> Don't use a lack of training as an excuse to not sell. If you don't know something, it's your responsibility to ask questions and seek out the training you need in order to get the job done.

Don't use a lack of training as an excuse to not sell. If you don't know something, it's your responsibility to ask questions and seek out the training you need in order to get the job done.

Should your employer do a better job training you? Probably. But if you want to keep the position you have, if you like your company and the product, if the customers are cool, and the compensation matches your goals, then take your own initiative. Don't sacrifice your success by claiming you don't have enough training. Ask for what you need. Show up, practice consistently, and get in the game every single day. You can't win if you don't play!

#2: Build your network every day.

The best salespeople dream and scheme about the people they want to do business with, and then they go after them. I'm not saying that having a database of prospects isn't a good thing, but if you're not getting leads delivered to you on a silver platter, you have to realize that every person you meet could be connected to your next sale. Opportunity lies around every corner. Networking is a way to stack the deck in your favor, even when it seems there aren't enough prospects to call on.

Volunteer to work with a charitable organization that means something to you. Attend business functions that include your ideal prospects. Join your local chamber of commerce. Each person you meet can provide a way for you to build your network and, in turn, your net worth. Every person matters. Be very intentional about building your relationships.

Pay close attention to your current client base as way to extend your network. A happy client can be a wonderful referral resource to create better leads—far more so than any list you could purchase. Ask your customers to introduce you to other people you'd like to know on LinkedIn. You'll have instant credibility when a mutual friend introduces you. This may seem obvious, but I believe LinkedIn is an untapped networking resource that many sales professionals don't use as effectively as they could.

You can also build your network through untapped leads. When I started my software sales job, I had a database full of leads left over from the salesperson I'd replaced. Admittedly, I knew very little about what I was doing at the time, but I did make several phone calls. I didn't get very far, so I quickly decided I needed another approach.

I decided to use the search feature of the database to identify leads that were in my state. Although Texas is a big place, I figured I could get in the car and go see these prospects, since the phone approach wasn't working very well. By doing this, I met a client in Austin who turned out to be my very best customer. And they stayed with me long after I left software sales and started my training company. They became one of the early clients at TrainerTainment and helped us grow during our first ten years of business.

My experience tells me that the strength of the network you build is contingent on how much you care about the people you serve. If you care enough, your network will stay with you for a lifetime.

#3: Stay in touch with the people who've bought from you in the past.

Not having enough people to call on isn't an excuse to stay stuck. If someone's bought from you before, then, by all means, keep those relationships alive! The event salespeople we coach at TrainerTainment call this PPO (Past Party Outreach) or PCO (Past Client Outreach).

If someone's already bought from you or your company, hopefully, they already love you. You already have a connection. Even if the original buyer has moved on and you have to reach out to a new person, you already have street cred because they purchased from you in the past. And if they didn't think the original experience was good, they now have someone new to work with. Take the shot. You have nothing to lose. So call on people who've bought from you before. They may be ready to buy again. If not, you haven't lost a single thing!

Working with past and current clients can also build your confidence. Ask them why they made the purchase or why they continue to buy from you or your company. You may find that what your clients say to describe your services is much more powerful than anything you could say to promote yourself.

When I started TrainerTainment, I reached out to people who had purchased capital equipment or done business with me in the past, and I asked them for testimonials. I was shocked at how kind people were, and I have to admit that I even wanted to buy from me when I read what they had to say!

My dear friend Joe Schumacker wrote, "There are many people who are experts in selling. There are a lot less who are also experts in sales management. The group gets very exclusive when you add training expertise to the skill set. Beth Standlee wins the Triple Crown."

#4: Ask for what you need, internally and externally.

Sometimes we whine. By *we*, I actually mean *me*. It's easy to sit back and whine that you don't have everything you need to close the deal—be that the support of your boss and the team, prospect lists, or marketing materials. If that describes you, then stop! If you don't have whatever "it" is, *take the initiative* to ask for whatever it might be, from whomever you think might have it! Nobody can read your mind—not the boss, not your customer, and not your co-workers. It's not their job to know what you need.

Remember the "best customer" I mentioned from Austin? Those guys were tough at times. Each year, I had to renegotiate the terms of our agreement. The owner was always a bit of a bully. I didn't like it. I didn't like the process, and I didn't like that they were trying to get me to come down on my price. It was awful. One year, I decided to state fully what I believed the locations needed the next year and what it would take financially and physically to get them to their new goals. I also decided if the conversation didn't go well, I'd simply pack up and go home. I got comfortable with an outcome that might include losing this customer. For me, that was super difficult. At the time, this client's business accounted for one-third of the total revenue for my company.

It was a meeting I'll never forget. We connected, I qualified, proposed the new year solution, and asked for the sale, which would cost more money than the previous year. The owner acted as if I'd asked him for his first-born child. I calmly put my computer away and packed up to leave.

My client asked, "Where are you going?"

"Home," I answered. "It looks like we're finished. I didn't mean to offend you with the offer, nonetheless, that's what it will take to get the job done next year. It doesn't seem to match up with what you want to pay."

For the first time, I was really brave enough to ask for what I needed. The vice president of operations stepped in and pointed out the success they'd had in working with me for the past three years. And in short order, they signed the deal. There were lots of hugs and a celebratory lunch following the one really tense moment—all because I had the courage to ask for what I needed.

This may sound harsh, but I know how easy it is to fall into the whiner's trap. My mentor calls it the oh-ain't-it-awful syndrome. Nothing good happens when you stay stuck in the ain't-it-awful whiner's ditch. You can waste a lot of unproductive time complaining about all the things you don't have.

It makes a lot more sense for you to take the lead like my friend and client Jenn in London, Ontario, Canada. She always asks for exactly what she needs. Jenn is one of the best sales professionals I've ever worked with. She's a hard-charging, do-it-now, event sales rep who was promoted to sales manager. Since we've worked together for a long time, I'm sure there have been occasions when she felt that they didn't need any more sales coaching. Regardless, she's never whined about it, at least not to me. But she does demand that we deliver the specific training they need in order to be successful, which keeps me and my team on our toes. It's a fantastic relationship that helps everyone grow. I admire Jenn's tenacity, and I'm confident she never complains that she doesn't have everything she needs to be successful.

#5: Be Your Own BEST Marketing Piece.

Sales and *marketing* are two sides of the same coin. People use these terms as if they are interchangeable, but they aren't.

Marketing products may include commercials, classic advertising outlets, a nice brochure, press releases, or events that provide introduction or exposure. *Marketing* is all about you, your product, and/or your service. However, *sales* is all about the customer. As a sales professional, I don't count on a marketing piece to do my selling.

Let me be clear: Marketing is a must. I want good-looking marketing materials. I want my web presence to create excitement about my product. I want social media to do its job to provide positive peer reviews and recommendations. But at the end of the day, I represent my company as the sales professional. It's how *I* show up and how *I* connect with the buyer that create positive word-of-mouth reputation and influence how my company is perceived.

Don't wait until you have the perfect brochure to start selling. Print temporary business cards if you must. If you're waiting on the marketing department to do your job for you, remember that it's not their job to do the heavy lifting of sales. Whenever you delay action, it gives your competition time to connect and sell to your prospective buyer. Don't let that happen. Figure out what marketing tools you can use right now and remember that *you* will make the best leave-behind impression.

#6: Data and CRM (Customer Relationship Management) Are Your Keys to Follow-Up.

There are many tools available today to help sales professionals stay alert and on top of their customer interactions. Heck, in the old days we used index cards, alphabetical dividers, and a file box to keep track of clients and client prospecting! The point is that you need a good system to track your data. I use the cloud-based CRM product, ZOHO, and there are many other robust systems available. The best system for you is the one you'll actually use.

Whatever CRM system you use, it needs to be online and accessible to everyone. Since selling is all about the client, then the more you can document and share with each other within your company, the better you can care for your customers.

If you don't have a CRM system, don't let that get in the way of your success. Ask your company to invest in a CRM system, or use Outlook or Gmail tools as a substitute. Document every interaction you have with a prospective buyer or client, and be sure to schedule the next follow-up appointment while you're with them. One friend, Phil Showler, schedules his next follow-up action or call while he's with the buyer (and maybe even his friends). In fact, I've heard him tell a prospect that he could count on hearing back from him until they served him with a restraining order!

The bottom line is that the deck is *not* stacked against you. When you change your attitude and approach, you can become a successful sales professional.

Follow-up and follow through are essential. Show up and win!

4

Help! I Sent Them an Email, But They Won't Get Back to Me

Guess what? I don't think relying on email alone is the best way to manage the sales process.

Let me tell you about Linda. I adore Linda. She's worked for a company we coach for many years. She's an amazing salesperson with a proven track record. She moves quickly. She shows up and is very good at developing relationships. But, like a lot of salespeople today, Linda relies too much on virtual communications. She's often told me, "I sent them an email to schedule an appointment to discuss their next event, but they won't get back to me!"

How can this be a surprise? Since the dawn of time, buyers haven't gotten back to sellers.

I have to put my foot down about communication. After all, the title of this book is *People Buy from People*! Of course, I know that people buy from Amazon, and online, and from catalogs, and with one click. However, online sales methods were built by people and for people, who had to learn to trust the virtual buying experience. People still want to talk to people when they're unsure of the process, when they have questions, or when things go wrong.

One-Way Communication

Email, Facebook Messenger, text messages, and even snail mail are different ways to push out information to a potential buyer. Think about that word *push*. Why would a sophisticated buyer want to deal with a pushy sales person?

Maybe you think I don't understand the soft-sell nature of an indirect tap on the shoulder through email. I assure you, I do. I use all forms of digital communications, but a long-lasting relationship can't be developed with one-way communication.

A long-lasting relationship can't be developed with one-way communication.

Here's the truth: If you're looking for a one-and-done sale, then you might be able to rely on email to bring in a one-time transaction. But that kind of buyer seeks out the lowest bidder (translation: lowest commission), and you can't expect any loyalty from them.

In *High Profit Prospecting*, Mark Hunter calls relying on mass email communication as the "spray and pray" method of prospecting. If that's what you want, great, but if you want to build real relationships that last a long time and result in great value for the buyer and larger profits for you, then keep reading.

They Won't Get Back to Me

Let's get back to Linda. The challenge for Linda—and for all of us—is that we misinterpret why prospects don't get back to us. We make assumptions, but there's no way to know what's true. Since both email and voicemail are one-way forms of communication, you can't actually know if the buyer received your message, so any conclusion you form is simply a guess.

Here are some common assumptions:

- They must not be interested.

- They probably selected a competitor.

- They think my product or service is too expensive.

- It's not a priority for them right now.

- I screwed up the presentation.

- AND my all-time favorite: They must not like me.

The truth is that it's not the buyer's job to get back to you. It's *your* job to connect with the buyer.

So how many times should you try to reach a prospect? It depends. How important is it for you to help them? What's the account worth to you and your company?

Here's what I know: Prospects don't get back to us because we aren't high enough on their list of priorities—yet. That's why it's so important to respond to an inbound call immediately. Never delay. Jill Konrath in *SNAP Selling* writes about "crazy busy buyers." She makes the astute observation that prospects are easily distracted, and the important initiative today will no longer be relevant tomorrow.

> The truth is that it's not the buyer's job to get back to you. It's your job to connect with the buyer.

I encourage you to be very open about the reasons why the client seems to be ignoring you. Don't make up stories about why they aren't getting back to you. If the buyer is an ideal client and you want to do business with them, then keep trying to connect. And don't count solely on email, voice mail, or any other type of one-way communication to do the job for you. Instead, find someone who knows the person and ask them to make an introduction. LinkedIn is particularly helpful in this type of situation.

> **Real communication is the foundation of a real relationship.**

Short of stalking the prospect, try to go to a networking event so you can meet this buyer in the flesh. Real communication is the foundation of a real relationship.

The Virtual vs. Personal Approach

Let's take a closer look at virtual communication as it relates to personally connecting. Many times, it isn't easy to personally connect with a buyer due to distance, time, and money. I've had to rely on the phone, email, and technology that allows for face-to-face meetings, like Zoom, Go-To-Meeting, and Google Hangouts.

Each time I think about the definition of *virtual*, I'm struck with the feeling that this kind of communication isn't real—or it's almost real, but not quite. And yet, I've experienced *really* getting in touch with people through LinkedIn, Facebook Messenger, and email.

---

vir·tu·al

1: being such in essence or effect though not formally recognized or admitted

2: being on or simulated on a computer or computer network

3: of, relating to, or using virtual memory

4: of, relating to, or being a hypothetical particle, whose existence is inferred from indirect evidence

Source: Merriam-Webster.com

Knowing how to best connect with buyers is complicated. We can send an email or text, place a phone call or snail-mail the potential buyer. However, since we know the first rule of the sales process is to *connect* with someone, it's easy to see how the virtual approach can create real crises in communication.

We're fortunate to have so much access to people. I love LinkedIn and use it to follow up with connections I've made in person. However, I don't use it for an initial connection unless I'm seeking a referral introduction (i.e., I know someone who knows the prospect I want to reach, and I ask my contact to introduce me to them virtually via LinkedIn.) I have instant credibility when a mutual friend connects me to a new prospect. When contact is made, you can bet I follow up as fast as possible with a phone call or even a face-to-face meeting when viable. I want to convert that cyber introduction into a more personal interaction as quickly as possible, so I can build a real foundation for the relationship.

At times, I've sent a Facebook message to someone I haven't been able to reach by email or on the phone. But it's important to note that I already knew this person. We wouldn't be connected on Facebook if we hadn't already interacted in some personal way.

Even though you can connect with someone virtually, I still believe that connection is indirect in nature. Relying on the "not real" world of virtual communication can foster a tremendous breakdown of intimacy in our relationships. I also think the average sales pro has a false sense that they're doing their job because they virtually reach out to someone through email. Remember, it's your job to *connect* with the buyer, not just attempt to communicate. Although you may be able to use email to cast a wider net to more people, more often, I think

Remember it's your job to connect with the buyer, not just attempt to communicate.

it's better to use email for follow up and for ongoing communication after you've made a real, personal connection.

Real Connection

The more personal the communication, the more likely you are to build a real relationship. The more connected the buyer is to you, the more likely they are to purchase.

Personal communication means there's back and forth communication between two parties. The most direct way to create sales is to get together with the buyer for a conversation. Here's how I rank the most efficient methods to build a personal relationship with a prospect and enjoy results you can count on:

1. **Meet the buyer face-to-face.** It's much easier to understand the other person when you gather all the interpersonal clues they reveal through body language, facial expression, tone, and words. The value of a handshake is real. Leaning in and listening to another person is meaningful. It's more difficult for a buyer to experience your "lean in" attitude when they're on the phone. And it's nearly impossible to communicate through email.

2. **Have a video meeting** where you can see one another. While body language may be a bit hidden, you can still read their facial expressions, their tone, and their words. I often have the sense of being in the same room or at the table with a prospect when we're on a Zoom video meeting.

3. **Pick up the phone.** I actually love using the phone and find it very efficient once a personal connection has been established. While reading body language and facial expressions is sacrificed on a phone call, hearing their tone is not. Tone plays such an important role

in communicating meaning. Many times, I've created confusion by firing off an email when I would've been better off having a quick phone call instead. And I have to admit, when I'm working from home, I sometimes take advantage of using the phone and make sales calls in my gym clothes!

4. **Use the indirect tools.** Finally, as a last resort, you can take advantage of all the written tools available such as email, Facebook Messenger, and text messages. But please know that if you rely solely on indirect, virtual methods of contact, you're less likely to sell to buyers who are interested in high-value, long-term relationships.

Case in Point

My friend Jim, who's one of the best sales guys I know, promotes a bowling tournament in Chicago called the Peterson Classic. People from all over North America bowl in this multiweek event.

Jim deals with squad captains, who organize and sign up the bowlers who participate in the tournament. Jim is ultimately accountable for overall sales of this event. From his home in Texas, he communicates, connects, and sells to people who live all over the country and want to bowl in this event in Chicago. It's a complicated, coordinated sales effort, to say the least.

Recently, Jim and I got into a great conversation as we talked about the frustrations of one-way communication through email. When he first received the assignment to promote the tournament, he had a ton of people he needed to connect with. So he did the most logical twenty-first century thing: He emailed everyone for whom he had addresses about the upcoming event. However, the Peterson Classic began in 1921, and many of the squad captains were senior citizens who didn't have email addresses. As it turns out, the most successful squads were those led by the people Jim contacted via phone or in person.

Jim understands how important connection is. He never forgets a face and rarely a name. The first year he was in charge of the tournament, he made several trips to Chicago because he understood how important it was to meet the squad captains face-to-face. He relies on the squad captains to sell out the event, so as he was organizing the tournament this year, he went to Chicago on different weekends than he did last year, so he could meet more of those captains in person. Jim's relationship with those key connectors determines the success or failure of the tournament. He talked about how many phone calls he's had with some of the non-email users and emphasized how high maintenance they are, but then he reminded me—or maybe himself—that those captains had the largest squads of the tournament.

Jim is highly connected. He's successful in sales not because of *who* or *what* he knows but because he builds lasting relationships with those people who are essential to him; those people *know him* and *trust him*. He makes everyone around him feel comfortable, and I happen to think comfort is a key ingredient of connection.

If you plan to have a successful sales career, then you have to get rid of any preconceived ideas that indirect, virtual forms of communication are the best—or only—way to connect with others. Create *real* relationships, that include *real* conversations, *really* often.

People buy from people, and when you take the time to cultivate high-value relationships where you're connected to one another, the sale you make today will often be the foundation for the long-lasting sales of tomorrow.

5

Stop Whining and Start Prospecting

rospecting—that's what sets you up to become a sales superstar and sets you apart from everyone else. To truly succeed in sales, there must be people who are willing to buy from you. It may sound silly, but what good is having a simple sales process if there are no buyers?

And when you know who your ideal buyer is, it's much easier to find your customer. While you may have several target markets, I'm sure that within each of those markets there are certain clients or customers you love more than others. It's a lot easier and much more fun to sell to those you love and who love you back. If it's not fun, I can't get very motivated to do it. With that in mind, let's identify your ideal buyer.

Identify the Ideal Buyer

Make a list of your favorite clients and write down the details about *what* made them an ideal prospect.

- At TrainerTainment, our ideal buyers are entrepreneurs who want help to improve their sales, service, or top-level business and leadership challenges. And in order to financially justify our services, it's more comfortable if their business has more than $1 million in annual revenue.

- We don't work with jerks; we like people who are obsessed with high performance.

- We pay our bills on time and expect our customers to pay us on time.

- We want to attract buyers who love to learn and are willing to be coached.

- Finally, their mindset should be to provide excellent service to their end users.

Being clear about the type of buyer we want has made a big difference in our results. I've always been very persuasive and can usually talk people into doing what I want them to do. But I've learned through the years that when I sell someone into my way of thinking, the results aren't very good. I'm much more successful when I make sure the potential buyer is an ideal buyer, so I try to connect with people who fit our ideal client profile. Then I listen to determine if they need what we sell. Starting with the ideal client makes my simple sales process much easier.

And, again, you must quit waiting for the business to come to you! If you spend at least 25 percent of your sales time prospecting, then the sky's the limit on the rewards that will follow. Incoming business-by-accident can't sustain your growth; you have to go out and find it. If you want to stand out from your competition, if you want more sales, and if you demand results that make your growth certain, then identify your ideal buyer and spend at least 25 percent of your sales efforts reaching out to grab this new business.

That's just the start. You must also have a particular attitude or mindset to prospect effectively.

Have a HIT Mindset

H = Habitual

Habitual prospecting must become second nature. It's something you will do *every* day without fail—no excuses. Mark your calendar with specific time blocks devoted to prospecting, and then treat that prospecting time as sacred. Turn off your email and don't take phone calls. This time is for prospecting alone.

The most successful periods in my sales career were those times I fanatically time-blocked my calendar to search for new business. Whether I was cold call-

> **Habitual prospecting must become second nature. It's something you will do *every* day without fail—no excuses.**

ing, networking, or following up on past or present leads, the commitment to capture new clients is what made the biggest difference in my commission check.

In his book *High Profit Prospecting,* Mark Hunter recommends spending 25 percent of your work week on new business development. I really appreciate that specific target of spending ten hours per week on prospecting. It helps me strategize and set goals. When I have a specific target, I can work on hitting it.

There are many benefits of strategically planning your new business outreach efforts:

- A consistent, weekly approach to prospecting keeps your sales pipeline full. The odds are in your favor when you have multiple opportunities waiting to close.

- Sales and business growth are a direct result of attracting new business.

- Prospecting gives you more control over that growth. It's very uncomfortable to just hang out and hope the next incoming call turns into a big sale.

- Prospecting is how you take charge of your own success, and it requires only 25 percent of your time.

Yes, you can create an enormous leap by spending only 25 percent of your time prospecting. And there's proof that this kind of focus works. Vilfredo Pareto, an Italian economist, noticed that 80 percent of all the land at the time was owned by 20 percent of the people. Since then, his observation has been expanded, and this 80/20 rule—or Pareto's Principle—has widespread application, even in sales.

I've seen numerous reports suggesting that 80 percent of an organization's sales can be attributed to 20 percent of the salespeople. I want you to be in that 20 percent! By dedicating 25 percent of your time toward developing new business, you can impact 75 to 80 percent of your overall results. Those are motivating odds; a little bit goes a long way!

In my early days when I was selling capital equipment, I inherited an ACT database of leads from the previous sales guy who covered my territory. I barely knew what to do. I'd never sold capital equipment, I was working remotely from home, and I didn't have an ideal client profile. My phone wasn't ringing, so I knew that if I wanted to keep this job, I had to make something happen. I decided my ideal customer would be someone who lived within driving distance of Fort Worth, Texas. I realize that's not a very sophisticated ideal client profile, but at the time, it served me well.

Even in my early days, I felt like I could make a better connection if I met the buyer in person. Although the "close to Fort Worth" criteria wasn't much to go on, I found a client in Bossier City, Louisiana, who agreed to see me!

I'll never forget that sales call. I was extremely nervous and talked to my manager during most of the drive over to Bossier. I didn't think I had the skill needed to demo the technology I was selling, but as it turned out, I didn't need to present a solution during that first call. After I gathered up my courage to leave the restroom in their building (yes, I was *really* nervous), I decided that my most important task was to connect with the buyer and learn how they were currently handling the issues that my product could improve.

In the end, that client did not purchase from me at the time. However, when I started my own company several years later, the needs of that client matched the services my training company provides. They signed up early on and have been long-term clients! It's true—*people buy from people*! And relationships can last a lifetime.

I'm so glad I decided to spend a small amount of my time calling people who were geographically close to me. Doors opened, the phone started ringing, and I experienced first-hand that a little bit of habitual effort can create great big results! Remember what Zig Ziglar said: "Motivation gets you started, but *habit* gets you there!"

I = Intentional

When you're intentional about doing something, that means you do it on purpose. You're deliberate. So intentional prospecting means that you prospect *on purpose*. It's not something you do on a whim or if you have time or if you're in the mood. You don't sit around and wait for a prospect to come to you. Your actions are intentional.

Prospecting allows you to create business that isn't there. You create something from nothing, and when you find sales that way, it's very rewarding. It's invigorating because you're the one who did it!

I refer to inbound business as "business by accident." That's when the phone rings and there's a ready, willing, and able buyer on the other end of the line. I love it. It's a lot easier. But that's not how the world of superstar sales works. Sales professionals make business happen *on purpose*.

One of the best things I've ever done is to create a daily sales journal and then share it with another salesperson on the team. Having an accountability partner increases the likelihood of being very intentional about the commitment you've made to reach any number of prospects each day. If you find that you're having trouble taking the initiative to make one more call or speak with one more person, then get more visible with your commitments. It works—I promise!

If you want to separate yourself from the crowd, then be intentional about finding business. Intentional prospectors determine how many people they'll reach on both a daily and a weekly basis. Making those connections ultimately determines how much you sell. Never settle for less than reaching your daily and weekly goals. And when you think your day is done, make one more call just for fun!

> Intentional prospectors determine how many people they'll reach on both a daily and a weekly basis. Making those connections ultimately determines how much you sell.

T = Tenacious

It's hard to keep up great habits and that spirit of intentionality if you aren't tenacious. When you look at the word *tenacious*, other words such as persistent, persevering, dogged, and stubborn, should come to mind. To me, tenacity is never giving up!

Buyers often have gatekeepers, and you must be tenacious to get past them. Sometimes you have to be brave to even reach out and shake hands with strangers. Some days it takes tenacity just to get out of bed. I'm either gifted or cursed (depending on how you look at it) with a quick-start way of being, so my own level of tenacity often makes up for bad habits because I simply jump in and start doing something.

In *The 5 Second Rule: Transform Your Life, Work, and Confidence with Everyday Courage*, a book by Mel Robbins, I found great inspiration that supports my HIT concept. When the author talks about confidence and everyday courage, it makes me feel tenacious. Robbins says that every time you have an idea or a goal or something you feel you should act on, your brain needs only seconds to talk you out of doing what you know you need to do. Her advice is to simply count backwards—5, 4, 3, 2, 1—and then DO IT. Blast off! She's a wonderful guide who can help with your own level of tenacity. I highly recommend you read her book if you find yourself struggling with prospecting.

How to Prospect

Now that you know your ideal buyer and have the mindset to prospect effectively, let's talk about how to prospect. Remember prospecting is NOT about you. It's all about the buyer! A lot of people equate prospecting with cold calling. I know very few sales professionals who actually like to cold call. I sure don't. However, I disagree with many sales gurus who have pronounced that the cold call is dead. I believe most cold call-type leads can be warmed up through a referral, through research, or through an introduction.

Regardless, prospecting is all about acquiring new business from an ideal buyer. And it must be part of your sales process in order to move from sales amateur to sales professional.

The cold call is one way to prospect, and when you do it, make sure you're calling on your ideal buyer.

In my Tupperware days, I had to cold call to build a new business because we'd relocated from Amarillo, Texas, to Fort Worth, and I had to rebuild my business from scratch. In the Tupperware organization, we didn't use the term *cold calling*; we called it *friend finding*. I didn't really like it, but if I wanted to keep selling Tupperware, it's what I had to do.

My ideal customer was a mom who stayed home, so I went around and knocked on doors in my neighborhood. Not many moms stayed home in the early nineties, and when someone actually answered the door, I had a pretty good shot at booking a party! That worked out great because it didn't take very many parties for me to meet lots of other people at those parties who were also ideal prospects. Guests of my "cold call" party hostesses turned out to be wonderful referral sources for new business, and my sales grew exponentially! For me, booking people at a party was a lot easier than friend finding (aka cold calling).

Other effective ways to prospect include renewals, rebooking, and referrals. It's important to communicate regularly with your existing clients. There are lots of statistics that prove that acquiring a new buyer is a whole lot more expensive than retaining an existing client.

From a sales perspective, it's always good to check in on your buyer. How are they enjoying your service or product? Is the value all they thought it would be?

I've found in a renewal or rebooking situation, it's much easier to sell any new or improved products or services to customers you already have. Think about it. Connecting with an existing client is easy. The relationship is established. When you stay in touch, you understand what's working and are able to intervene if something isn't. Ideally, you're able to identify additional needs, which helps build new sales with an old client. Finally, great existing relationships help open new doors, which is what prospecting is all about.

When it comes to referrals, connect with all the people you know—including your current clients—and research how they might connect you to others. Building a solid prospect list from referrals is a great way to get your foot in the door.

One of my favorite questions to ask people who have purchased from me is, "Who else do you know that might benefit from our services?"

We coach a lot of event salespeople, and in our referral coaching sessions, we ask them to ask people who have held recent events in their facility: "Who else in your company might enjoy an event just like the one you all had?" I've found that people are generally happy to help, especially when they value what you sell. You never know which relationship could hold the key to your next big sale.

Let me share an "old school" referral example. Way back when—for only ninety days—I sold Lincoln-Mercury cars. It was exciting at first, and I sold cars to all my friends and family. They then told all their friends and family, and I sold a few more vehicles. However, I quickly learned that the fun factor in car sales was going to be a big challenge for me. After I exhausted what I believed were all my new business resources, I was relegated to walk-in prospects—and they were always in "buyer beware" mode. That didn't work for me because I didn't like being in an automatic adversarial role with a potential client. I simply wanted to help get him or her into a new car.

Although I was reasonably good at the job, I knew it wasn't for me. I sold thirty cars in ninety days and was tenacious enough not to fall prey to the average statistics, which said that most new car salespeople quit in their first ninety days. For my own peace of mind, I did go to work on day ninety, but I resigned by lunchtime!

Even though selling cars wasn't for me, I learned how easy and important it is to tap into the resources of the people you know. Look around. Who do you know who knows someone you need to know? This is the straightest path to effective referral prospecting.

My "new school" of thought keeps me searching when I think I've run out of ideal leads. LinkedIn is one of my favorite resources to expand my prospect list. I often find I'm only one person removed from my ideal buyer. And it makes sense for the person who knows both of us to introduce us to one another. In those cases, my credibility is raised because I've been referred by a mutual friend.

I suggest that you link with every new person you meet. Send them a note that reminds them how you met, and tell them you'd like to keep in touch. DO NOT try to sell them anything during this first outreach!

Sales amateurs pitch their products to every connection. Don't make that rookie mistake. Don't start pitching to an ideal buyer too soon. It's easy to fall into the trap of talking about yourself and your product. It is, after all, what you know best. But the truth is, most people try to avoid those who talk only about themselves. Instead, ask questions and find out more about them.

Here's a little trick I use: When I'm prospecting, I like to pretend I'm a journalist rather than a salesperson. This gets me focused on the other person and takes the focus off of me. Try it yourself! Once you perfect this journalistic prospecting approach, you'll find that buyers invite you to talk about your product. It may sound counter-intuitive, but I promise if you implement the rest of the sales process as explained in the following chapters, you'll turn more prospects into buyers, who will refer you to their friends and family. In turn, your sales will soar.

> Here's a little trick I use: When I'm prospecting, I like to pretend I'm a journalist rather than a salesperson.

From Amateur Seller to Sales Professional

I had the pleasure of coaching a young woman named Cheryl who sold events at an entertainment venue in eastern Louisiana. When we started, she was new to sales—only one week under her belt—but she was enthusiastic enough to start visiting potential buyers before she had any idea what she was doing. Talk about taking initiative! I had to admire that kind of enthusiasm. We talked about the PCQPC approach as the foundation for her initial training.

Cheryl was a quick study and an avid learner. She immediately recognized that she wasn't really selling but was simply dropping off information to any and all potential buyers. But the simple truth was that she wasn't getting any results. Come to find out, Cheryl had some limiting beliefs about how she saw herself, as well as the overall role of the salesperson. Her core belief was that selling for a living was shady and salespeople were smarmy. She even thought having a different, non-sales title would help her quest for new business. I told her that any type of dressed-up title would feel insincere to the buyer.

The only mistake Cheryl had made was in her approach, which had been self-focused. When we planned how she could "interview" her prospects versus what she'd been saying, she exclaimed, "I did it all wrong!" I said that her approach wasn't necessarily wrong, and if she wanted to knock on many, many doors before she closed a sale, she could keep doing it that way.

My journalistic way of prospecting was simply different, and I think it's easier. The very next week, Cheryl took on the role of prospecting journalist, and it proved to be much more successful. She had fun, and it was easier to get the conversation going when she focused on the buyer rather than trying to impress them with her stuff. In fact, she booked several events within the first three weeks as a new salesperson—the direct result of trying a new, client-centered way of business prospecting!

Here's my bottom line: professional salespeople never stop prospecting.

6

I Found a Prospect.
What Do I Do NOW?

aking a *connection* is the logical first step in any healthy
sales encounter. Although some may argue that there's
no one-size-fits-all method for selling, I've never heard
anyone disagree with this fact: It's much easier to sell to someone
if they feel connected to you. If you haven't made a connection,
you haven't earned the right to talk about your product or service.

As a consumer, I prefer to buy from friends. Why is that?
It's because I—like most people—feel more comfortable buying
from someone I trust, and my trust level is much higher with
the people I know. Connection provides the foundation for
trust. It creates comfort for both the buyer and the seller, and
it makes it possible to develop a relationship that can last a long
time. Connection is *critical* to the entire sales process.

You can be assured that you've connected with someone
when you've established common ground and created comfort
for yourself and the buyer.

Common Ground

Most people think that connecting with someone means building rapport or finding common ground. I agree. As a concept,
common ground means to discover a shared interest or opinion

that you can build on. And yet, many salespeople skip the connection step and start talking about themselves and the stuff they sell. I see that every day: "Hi, I'm Sam the Salesman and boy have I got a deal for you!" No, no, NO! You must start with a common-ground approach.

Alec Greven, a one-time eight-year-old author, laid it out best in his book, *How to Talk to Girls*. Alec says that no girl likes a show-off. The best way to approach a girl is to "Say hi. If she says hi back, you are off to a good start!" If a child can understand this on such a fundamental level, you can, too. I consider Alec's book a must-read sales primer for anyone who wants to become a good salesperson.

Before you meet your prospect, do your homework. Find out about their business and research them online until you discover something you have in common or something that could be a conversation starter. LinkedIn is a great resource for this kind of research, and I encourage you to look them up. This isn't stalking; it's common practice between business professionals.

> **Before you meet your prospect, do your homework. Find out about their business and research them online until you discover something you have in common or something that could be a conversation starter.**

When you meet face-to-face with a prospect, you can also find common ground as you observe their surroundings, listen to their words, and pay attention to your own intuition. Touch creates connection, and perhaps there are some other woo-woo ways I don't know about. For example, I once walked into a prospect's office and noticed he had Arkansas Razorback paraphernalia on the top of his bookshelf. Without any thought, I reached out to shake his hand and very naturally asked, "Are you from Arkansas?" He was, and bingo! We'd found common ground. If he'd said no, there was still a good chance that he'd have a story to tell me about his Razorback swag, and we would've had a deeper connection than before I'd walked into his office.

It may seem silly to make a big fuss over a simple handshake, but the touch that comes with a handshake can physically create connection. When you physically touch someone, you have the opportunity to create a calm, empathetic connection and even build trust.

Listen. You must listen! Connection can't happen when you're too focused on your next move. You can't possibly hear the words a prospect is using or even get a clue from your own intuitive sense when you're up in your own head.

Many times, in many relationships, connection gets lost because we're so focused on what to say or do next. We may not even really hear what the other person says as we formulate our next sentence.

Be patient and *present.* Understand that genuine connection is an outgrowth of excellent communication. A big clue as to whether or not you're getting it right is if there's a nice flow of back and forth between the buyer and the seller.

Please note, I don't want you to confuse finding common ground with idle, time-wasting chit chat. Neither you nor the buyer has a minute to waste talking about the weather or other useless information.

Sometimes salespeople can be overly friendly and talk, talk, talk when they first meet a prospect. I, too, can become quite chatty when I get nervous. That may work if the person you're talking to is also anxious about the meeting. However, being a nervous, overly friendly, chatty Cathy is usually not a great way to find common ground. A better method is to introduce yourself, listen, observe, and then speak. In fact, if you're dealing with the kind of person who likes to get straight to the point,

I promise that you'll establish more rapport by talking about how you want to get straight to the point rather than by talking about anything else.

Other ways to find common ground include giving a sincere compliment, thanking them for seeing you, or even exchanging a simple smile. Lean in toward the buyer, whether you're in person or talking on the phone. Observe everything when you meet them in person.

I believe you need to be part journalist, part detective, and part psychologist to become an excellent "connecter" sales pro. This may sound like a tall order, but when you lean in, listen, and observe others, it's much easier to connect at a level that builds the trust you need to move into the buyer/seller relationship. Be *interested* rather than *interesting*.

Phone Work

If you're trying to find common ground on the phone, you need to rely on your previous research—which means that you must have done the research—and what you hear them say. Observe the prospect's *words* and *tone* and listen well.

Tony Robbins encourages matching and modeling in order to fall in step with the other person. With that in mind, I pay close attention to the pace at which the prospect speaks. I talk fast if they're speaking fast, slowly if they're speaking slowly, and more loudly or softly depending on their volume. I try to match the buyer's speech pattern because when I do, something happens subconsciously in both our brains, and we identify as being like one another in this voice-matched exchange.

For example, let's say you're from Boston, and you make a call to Texas. If the person on the other end of the line pronounces the letter r just like you do, then there will be no doubt that you have something in common! The Bostonian pronunciation is unique, and that alone can establish common ground that can, ultimately, lead to connection.

In order to find common ground, I suggest you do one more thing: Develop your psychology skills by learning more about people's personalities. People tend to communicate in the manner they prefer, and that works well as long as you're dealing with someone who's just like you. But there are at least three other personality types who have needs that are very different from yours. When you learn to communicate with others *at their level,* you won't only become a common-ground sales pro, you'll become a better friend, parent, lover, and person!

The DISC assessment is my favorite method for learning more about personality styles. According to DISC, there are four personality profiles. Within those four types you have people who may be very outgoing and direct (extroverted) or more indirect (introverted). Another general characteristic people fall into is they are either more social and people-centric, or they may be more selective and discerning when it comes to people. With that knowledge, you can probably guess that many salespeople are in the extroverted, people-centric category.

The differences in personality style are profound and can impact how we relate to one another. Salespeople who fit in the extroverted category can sometimes misjudge the quiet introvert as someone who's uninterested or even aloof when, in actuality, they're simply processing the communication internally rather than externally. They are being them, and you are being you.

It's good to know about the different styles up front because that knowledge can help you connect and communicate with others in a way that's comfortable for them. I encourage you to improve your connections by learning more about the DISC way of understanding others. I've given a very simple thirty-thousand-foot overview of DISC, but there's so much more to learn. I credit my ability to connect well with others to being exposed to DISC in my early twenties! My hope is that you'll dive in right away and begin to expand your understanding of others today. Go to https://www.thediscpersonalitytest.com.

Comfort

When people are comfortable with you, it's easy to connect. I bet you've had the experience where you met a stranger, and in minutes, you felt like you'd known them forever. You just clicked, or they reminded you of an old friend. You were immediately comfortable with someone, and trust was built.

But that's not the way things usually work in sales. Many people have a natural negative bias when it comes to salespeople. If you can figure out what to do to create comfort for the buyer and yourself, you'll make a successful connection, which allows you to take the next step in the sales process. I've said it before and will repeat it again: You cannot, should not, and I hope will not start talking about yourself until you've first made a solid connection.

Establishing common ground can increase the comfort level. However, you must also work on your ability to tap into *your own comfort* in any situation. It's easy to get the jitters, whether you're young in your sales role or are meeting a new prospect for the first time.

One way to get more comfortable is to *prepare* and *practice*. Research your potential client. Practice what you'll say to them over and over again. I have found that when buyers know you've done your homework and are prepared for the meeting, their respect creates a sense of confidence and comfort for everyone.

We've all experienced the lack of connection with telemarketers. For example, if someone calls me and asks to speak to Helen Standlee, I know they don't know me. Yes, Helen is my first name, but nobody calls me that. Clearly, they haven't done their research. Don't be that person! Research the prospect and call them by their appropriate name.

Understand what role the person plays in their company. Be curious about their contribution to the buying decision. A simple question to ask is, "How long have you worked for the company?"

Comfort builds trust. It helps alleviate difficult situations. Build that comfort and trust by learning all you can about the buyer before you meet.

Further, you must be confident in your product knowledge; if not, you'll be all up in your head trying to think about what you need to say when it's finally your turn to talk about yourself and your product. And if that happens, you won't be listening to the prospect. You'll miss all the good stuff they're sharing with you.

> Comfort builds trust. It helps alleviate difficult situations. Build that comfort and trust by learning all you can about the buyer before you meet.

Fear is one of the main reasons why we get nervous and uncomfortable. Many years ago, a sales mentor of mine, Charlene Goodson, was listening in on a sales call. I was extremely nervous because I wanted to impress Charlene. I needed to "sell" the person I was trying to connect with to have a meeting with me right away. My discomfort manifested itself in a very fast phone call that ended abruptly. The buyer literally said nothing. I didn't breathe for at least two minutes as I hurried through my script!

Charlene was terrific. She looked at me and said, "Wow, that was fast! You gave good information, but there was no way the prospect could get a word in edgewise. Are you OK?"

That call happened a long time ago, and my heart still races a little when I think of it. I had to find a way to let go of the fear. Breathing is a great place to start. Deciding to slow down before you get on the phone is a good idea, too.

It's impossible to anticipate every sales scenario. No matter how much you prepare, you can count on things happening that you don't expect and can't plan for. My advice is to exchange your *fear* for *curiosity*. Watch for the surprises. Welcome them. When the unknown pops up, have fun with it! I promise you'll learn something you can use next time.

> No matter how much you prepare, you can count on things happening that you don't expect and can't plan for. My advice is to exchange your fear for curiosity.

I think it's charming to watch children be naturally curious about their world, and that's helped me to tap into my own comfort level on sales calls. To get rid of my fear, I like to play a little trick on myself that's fun and works for me. I pretend the prospect is five years old. Seriously! This helps because when I calm my own discomfort and become a little more childlike in my curiosity, I can better support the buyer who may not feel naturally comfortable in the situation either.

Your client can't get comfortable if you don't get yourself to a relaxed, or at least an optimistic, state. When you're comfortable, you can focus on the prospect and you'll naturally quiet the noise in your head that contributes to separation and a lack of trust—two things you definitely don't want.

I wish I could offer you a fail-safe way to know how to connect with prospects 100 percent of the time, but the reality is that connecting will be different for each person you meet. I don't think there's a perfect script to guarantee connection.

A lot of people want email to do the job for them; but remember, email is a one-way form of communication. Connection implies there's a back-and-forth exchange between two people. A great subject line in a well-written email might pique someone's interest, but trust isn't built until real connection happens.

I can show you how *not* connecting works. I was working our trade-show booth at a big show and had just finished a great conversation with a prospective buyer. My enthusiasm carried over to the next person who walked up to our booth. I completely forgot my own sales process and began the blah, blah, blah of all we could do to help them grow their event sales. No "Hello, I'm Beth, and you are…" Nope, I just started pitch-slapping them. My leftover excitement from the previous customer created a false sense of confidence that I projected onto this new person, whom I didn't know a thing about!

When I took my first breath, the uncomfortable customer interrupted and said, "What makes you think we have a problem with our event sales?"

I'm pretty sure I turned many shades of red. In an instant, I knew I had wasted this guy's time and lost my chance to develop a new relationship.

In a way, I'm glad it happened because I'll never ever forget that feeling. On the rare occasion that I forget to connect first, I remember the embarrassment of that day.

I admit, I'm always busy, and sometimes it seems easier to just get down to business. But I know that if I don't make a connection, the sale is reduced to a price-based transaction. So I usually slow down and remember that it's impossible to have a comfortable, trust-filled relationship without connecting first!

I wasn't able to recover that bad booth experience, but now when a wall goes up and connection is blocked, I go back to the beginning and focus first on finding common ground and creating a comfortable environment so we can get to know one another better.

What If You Have Trouble Connecting?

There are times when connecting may seem impossible. Once in a while, I bump into someone with whom there's just no common ground. I can get tripped up and even feel little awkward in these moments. I usually discover this type of client wasn't a good fit to begin with. Or the awkwardness could be a signal that we have a personality conflict, and it may be better for another sales rep to handle the account. In those cases, I pass them on to someone else.

But what if you're connected to someone in the organization, and they aren't the one making the buying decisions? Don't dismiss them! Your ability to connect with the buying *influencer* may be just as important as your ultimate connection to the decision maker. Influencers have power, and you should leverage that relationship. They can help you understand the job criteria, so you're fully prepared when you eventually meet the decision maker.

For example, at TrainerTainment, we hired a wonderful team member a while back, but she had to sell herself inside the organization before she got to me. Fortunately, she understood the sales process, and while she didn't connect with me (the ultimate decision maker) at first, she reached out to an influencer on our team. It took time, probably more time than she wanted it to take, but ultimately her internal contact encouraged me to talk to her—and the rest is history. As busy as I am, we—the company—could have missed a huge opportunity if she hadn't come at it another way. Thank goodness she persisted.

There are so many ways to connect:

- Being physically present with others builds comfort.

- Curiosity is a must.

- Look for common ground.

- Reach out to others because you genuinely want to help them.

- Find things you agree on up front.

- Be congruent with your words and actions.

Some say, "Fake it till you make it." But I say, "Be you, because others will know if you aren't!"

Remember that you have two ears and one mouth, so listen twice as much as you talk. Build engagement and trust through confidence and enthusiasm.

Remember people want to buy from their friends, and it's your job to create enough comfort so the buyer believes in and is connected to you.

And remember, this connection might take two minutes or two hours or even days! Invest yourself in the process. It's practically impossible to sell things to people when you have no connection with them.

7

How to Qualify the Buyer So They'll Invite You to Talk About Your Stuff

Here's the thing: It's going to take a lot of discipline to avoid pitching too soon.

What you sell is worth nothing until you know how it serves your buyer. You can talk endlessly about features and benefits, but that's not what gets buyers excited. It's the buyer's *perceived value* that counts. Before you start pitching your product, you must build its value first.

Just for fun, let's compare sales to a social setting. Say you were attracted to someone at a party. You wouldn't run up to him or her and start talking about how wonderful it would be for them to date you, would you? Of course not! However, in sales we often lead with our products, our "stuff." It's a total turnoff, just like it would be to push yourself on someone who doesn't know you yet.

Picture your prospect as that other person at the party. It will help you to restrain yourself, so you can move through the qualification process.

Remember that qualifying your prospect is a process! You must have the discipline to execute the entire process.

It can be tempting to simply discover one or two pieces of

key information, decide you have everything you need to know, and then move in for the kill—and it's far too soon. And you'll lose the sale.

Exercising restraint doesn't slow down the sales process; it speeds things along because you'll learn what you need to know before you propose the solution. You'll have a solid framework to help you discover if you need to do more work before you ask for the order. You'll have the confidence to know whether or not you'll close the sale. Although this step is where you may spend most of your time with a buyer, it makes all the other steps go more quickly—especially compared to how you may have done things in the past.

During this part of the sales cycle, the customer should do most of the talking. Check yourself! If you're talking more than your buyer, you can assume that you're pitching too soon. Truthfully, I catch myself doing this all the time. I have to back up and focus on the five things I need to know before I start that product presentation, which I'll tell you about later in the chapter.

Think of yourself in a different role

Sales is about being truthful with your prospects, but you can stretch things a little with yourself to become a more effective salesperson. I advocate pretending, or to "act as if." One sure way to help you break the habit of talking about yourself is to pretend you're in a different profession. Try replacing your sales hat with any of these other professions. In other words, act as if you are a:

- **Journalist.** Professional news gatherers ask questions. They're consumed with curiosity. Some would even say they're nosey. During the qualification part of the sales process, being nosey is good!

- **Detective or private investigator.** If you have a sneaky streak, then the detective persona is for you. Sneaking around looking for clues to close is so much better than the "me, me, me" approach most salespeople take. A great clue is when you find insight about the pain the buyer has and know that pain can be solved by your product. Learn all you can about the buyer. Ask questions about their role in the company. Uncover every clue available to figure out how the buyer would be positively affected by owning your product. This approach helps you feel much more confident when it comes time to propose a buying solution.

- **Talk show host.** Personally, I love this one. It's fun to imagine that you're interviewing a VIP on your very own sales channel! The buyer is always a celebrity in my book, and I'm committed to conducting the very best interview. As the host of this sales show, I want my buyer to feel extremely important, and I want to learn as much as I can to keep them coming back to my show again and again!

- **Consultant or counselor.** In chapter 1, I said, "Great selling is about helping others." And I often feel like I'm counseling the buyer. In the qualification phase, I want to discover the challenges or opportunities the prospect is facing, so my questions are buyer-centric. I lean in physically, listen, and let the other person talk. Then I ask questions that will let them know I'm trying to help them, as well as make a sale.

Have fun with this! Try out one of these four "alternate" personas to build your curiosity sales muscles. When you become skilled at the qualifying process, you'll start doing business with the right people, you'll gain confidence, and buyers will be inspired to work with someone who's keenly interested in them—you!

How do you know when you know enough?

Now that you're in the qualification zone, you need to learn how to ask the right questions. I believe that, no matter what you sell, there are five pieces of information you need to help you present a solution that the buyer can't resist. It's a bold statement, but I've used this process to sell plastic bowls, cars, capital equipment, events, and training. I believe you'll be able to translate the concepts for your business, too. We'll explore each item individually, and I'll give examples based on selling events.

> No matter what you sell, there are five pieces of information you need to help you present a solution that the buyer can't resist.

trainer ainment
fun training | serious results

Am I Ready to Present?

- O Logistics
- O Hot Buttons
- O Competition
- O Decision Maker
- O Tolerance for Spend

"The discipline of waiting to present until you have all the boxes checked off will increase your close ratio."

Beth Standlee

The Five Things

Each of these five items can help you design the best solution for your buyer. Remember, **people buy from you based on what *they* want, not what you have to sell.** So how do you find out what they want? Start with a conversation with the buyer—that's the easiest way. Make them the most important person in your world, and probe to discover the answers to the five essential buying categories below.

1. Logistics

Logistics are the basic bricks that make up every sale. They include things like how many, when, what size, how soon, etc. Anything sold has fundamental elements, and most sales amateurs think this is all they need to know to create a sales order. However, I want you to *resist pitching* until you have more information than just the logistics, although I have to admit, sometimes pitching when you have only the who, what, where, when, and how many may work.

Sometimes you can ask a couple of probing, logistical questions—or the customer may even tell you what they think they want—you then propose a solution, and, just like that, the client buys. Boom! You're a sales superstar. This outcome is what I call *intermittent reinforcement.* The same thing happens at a slot machine. You put your money in, pull on the one-armed bandit or push a button, and boom! Once in a while you get a return on your investment. But it's still a gamble. As a matter of fact, I'm pretty sure that slot machines don't really pay off in the long run! The same is true if you decide to pitch when you only know the basics. As much as I like to gamble and play slot machines, I don't like to gamble with my work effort.

The difference is that when I play my favorite slot machine—video poker—I do it for entertainment. I know I'm gambling. When I put in effort at work, I want to be *certain* of a return.

Sample Logistics Questions:
I deal primarily with event salespeople, so my best questions are:

- How many people are planning to attend the event?
- Were you thinking of a daytime or evening event?
- Weekend or weekday?
- Are you interested in food and fun?
- Have you been to our location in the past?
- What did you think?

If you're ready to stop gambling with your sales results, let's look beyond the logistics of the buy and focus on the other four key pieces of information you need from the buyer, so you'll hit the jackpot when it's time to propose the best solution.

2. Hot Buttons (The WHY of Their BUY)

I love to ask the buyer, "If your event were perfect, what would it look like?" When I lead with that question, the event planner frequently answers the other questions without my having to ask. Depending on his or her personality, they may describe the event in such wonderful detail that I'll know when they want it to occur, how many will attend, what they want, the experiences they've liked or disliked in the past, and whether or not I'm talking to the decision maker. They may even tell me how much money they want to spend.

I promise, the "if your event were perfect" question is magic, and you can ask this type of question in every sales field:

Real estate: "If you could have your ideal home, what would it look like?"

Financial planning: "If you could paint your retirement years perfectly, what would they look like?"

Fitness center: "If you could predict the ideal outcome for your time spent in the gym, what would that look like?"

Tupperware or any other direct sales: "When you think about perfection when it comes to *food prep/storage (accessories, makeup)*, what does that look like?"

Get the idea? It took me years to realize that most people didn't know what I was talking about when I referred to "hot buttons." It's simply this: What's really important to the buyer? What turns them on? Then it occurred to me that I needed to update my terminology: we must **learn the *why* of the *buy*.** Why someone wants or needs something gives us clues about what we should discuss when we prepare to present, pitch, or propose our product.

It's been said that people purchase based on emotion and then later justify their purchase with logic. It's during that logical phase that buyers experience remorse. I've found that when we get connected to the *why* of the buy, we can reinforce that *why* during the presentation phase. While the *why* is much more linked to the emotion of the buy, the presentation can also reinforce the logic of making a great decision.

I like to connect the emotion to the logic *before* they make a buying decision. I never want the customer to have remorse about purchasing from me. Psychologically, understanding why someone wants or needs to purchase your products or services can be the single difference in whether or not they follow through. With that said, don't start pitching yet. There are three more key pieces of information to gather.

Sample Hot Buttons / Why They Buy Questions:
Because I deal primarily with event sales people, the best questions are:

- Tell me more about your event.

- Is this a special occasion?

- Are you hoping to have a team-building event? Recognition/reward?

- Fun day/night out?

And, of course, my favorite question of all:

- If this event were perfect, how do you see it coming together? What are the two or three most important factors for you and your people?

3. Competition

I used to hate to learn about my competition. I'm actually quite competitive, but in sales, I'd get nervous and even jealous when I thought I was competing for business. It may sound silly, but it was something that held me back. In a world of sales where you either win the business or learn something because you missed the sale, knowing who won the sale instead of you can be a critical component in winning the next piece of business. With that knowledge, I figured that knowing who the competition was before I lost the sale might give me a clue how to win more!

Tom Searcy, co-author of *Whale Hunting: How to Land Big Sales and Transform Your Company*, helped me understand and transform my negative resistance to learning about my competition. What struck me is how simple his approach was. I immediately got comfortable with asking a potential buyer, "If you don't buy from me, what will you do?" I'm paraphrasing a bit, but honestly, I've used those very words. The secret is to wait. Stay silent until they respond. Remember the two ears/one mouth thing! Practice breathing and simply listening when you ask this question.

I'm pretty sure that most sales folks are competitors at heart. And while it's easier to pretend we're the only game in town, it's rare that the sophisticated buyer doesn't consider several options. So I think it's better to know the enemy than not. I'm in no way suggesting you bash your competition. Please don't do that. You'll usually lose points for that kind of behavior.

I am suggesting that you sell the benefits of your product compared to the other option. Point out the differences in a way that builds your company up rather than tearing the competition down. Although this may seem like a softer approach, I prefer to think of it as respectful.

I also try to operate from an "abundance mentality," which suggests there's enough for everyone. It's my job as a sales professional to create connection, qualify the buyer's needs at the highest level, make the best case I can for my product, and finally ask for the business. When I do that, I have a damned good shot at winning the business, no matter who the competitor is.

When I play the game at the highest level, I believe I can win. I have to admit that my feathers still get a little ruffled when a buyer asks me how I'm different from my competitor or whom I consider my primary competitor. However, I smile and say, "I'm so glad you asked me." I answer in a way that suggests that I don't really have *competitors*, but rather people who do things differently than our company. I point out how our company is different and then get back on track with my own questions that address why they might buy from me rather than someone else. I want as much information as I can gather to craft a presentation that specifically highlights why our company is the best choice. My favorite qualifying competitor questions are listed below.

Sample Competitor Questions:
Remember, I deal primarily with event salespeople, so my best questions are:

- How do you normally decide where to hold an event like this?

- What else are you considering if you don't hold your event here?

- Where have you held events in the past? (this could also help you understand the fifth qualification step of tolerance for spend)

- When you went to (fill in your competitor's name), what did you like/dislike about the experience?

- What made you choose them in the first place and what motivated you to give us a shot this time?

4. Talk to the Decision Maker

Here's a qualification question that trips me up on occasion. I make friends easily and often times assume I'm talking with the decision maker. I'll feel so good about the encounter, that I forget to ask if there's anyone else involved in the decision-making process. This is an amateur mistake that has cost me a lot of money in lost sales and, more importantly, lost time. And time is the most valuable asset in the sale professional's life.

I'm not saying that you should spend zero time with people who simply influence the buying decision. Depending on what you sell, there may be several people who need to buy in before you get to the decision maker. I've learned to never alienate anyone. I give respect to everyone in the organization. You can never be sure who holds the key to the decision maker's office, and you can't afford to miss the opportunity to learn more from anyone in the chain of command. Since people buy from people, knowing several influencers in an organization can help you get to the decision maker.

The challenge can be difficult to overcome when you can't get in front of the actual buyer. You have to trust your advocate—who isn't really the final decision maker—to sell your product.

While a sales advocate is very important, they're rarely as qualified as you are to sell your stuff.

Here are a series of questions and methods to use to get in front of the decision maker.

Sample Decision Maker Questions:

- "Do you manage all the details of this purchase, or are there other people helping you?" I love this question because it assumes the person you're talking with has the ability to make the decision. When I ask this question in this way, the buyer lets me know if they need to talk with someone else, if they're part of a fact-finding committee, or if the buck stops with them. It doesn't necessarily mean the CFO or the owner may not still need to sign off on the purchase, but if they indicate that they alone can make the decision, it means they're pretty sure of their influence.

If two or more people are part of the decision-making process, I ask:

- "How do you and your partner normally make decisions like this?" One time, I was talking to one-half of a partnership and everything was going great. However, I was acutely aware of the fact that I needed to be in front of both buyers. So when I said, "How do you and your partner normally make decisions like this?" his answer was, "Over lunch." It was a great opening for me to respond, "Great, how would Thursday work for ya'll?" And just like that, I got to the next step, which included my selling my products to both buyers without relying on one partner to sell it to the other.

5. Tolerance for Spend

I intentionally position price as the final step in the qualification process. Sometimes people—the buyer or the seller—want to talk about money up front. I find when the financial piece is the primary part of the conversation, there's not much room for understanding the full value of the purchase.

If money is the main focus of the conversation, you're probably selling a commodity or are involved in a transactional sale. When money is the primary topic, whatever you're selling is usually, to the buyer, too expensive. In my sales coaching experience, I've encountered salespeople who believe their primary objection from buyers is always around price. With few exceptions, I find that the salesperson brought up price too early in the conversation.

A sales amateur will ask, "What's your budget?" early in the sales qualification step. Talking about price up front is a sure way to "cheap sell" or compete in a way that's not profitable for the company or for you. Don't get me wrong, price is important, but it's not usually the most important part of the sale. What matters most is the value of what you're selling and its relationship to the price. You have time to make your case once you understand what's most important to the buyer.

Let me prove my point. If you've ever bought a car, you might have had this experience. You walk up and a salesperson welcomes you and usually does a pretty good job connecting. And then it happens, invariably, near the beginning of the conversation, they ask a question that sounds something like this, "How much money are you looking to spend?" I want to scream at them and answer, "GIVE ME THE BIGGEST, BADDEST CAR YOU HAVE FOR THE LEAST AMOUNT OF MONEY, DUMBASS! And by the way, IT'S NONE OF YOUR BUSINESS."

Fortunately, I've never said those words out loud. But don't you see what I mean? It's not a smart approach. If budget is the primary issue, the prospect will let you know. Otherwise, focus on connecting and understanding the *why* of someone's buy, if the person you're dealing with can make the decision, who you're competing with, and the basic logistics of the purchase. Then and only then is the price conversation relevant.

It's important to learn what people want to spend, but any time I've asked about budget, the buyer typically holds back, lowballs the figure, or they out-and-out lie. The buyer's job is to get a fair deal. The seller's job is to understand all the needs of the buyer, including tolerance for spend. But honestly, when the buyer is connected to the seller and they love the brand and the product, then the price winds up being pretty low on the list of priorities. When all things are equal, the seller, the brand, and the product are always more important than the price. A full understanding of the first four qualification items make handling price issues much easier.

People change their behavior and thinking by first changing their language. So from now on, as a sales professional, separate yourself from budget and begin to try and understand what the buyer's tolerance for spend really is. It doesn't help you to have the game playing discussion about budget that happens in negotiation. Don't play games when it comes to the value of your product. If there's integrity in your pricing then you have a responsibility to your company to sell the product or service for the price that's been established, and you owe it to the buyer to help them understand the value of your product as it relates to their needs.

Sample Tolerance for Spend Questions:

- How do you decide what to spend on an event like this? (Substitute the word *products, services*, etc., for the word *event.*)

- What have you spent on events like this in the past? (You may also learn more about a previous competitor with this question.)

The biggest benefit of getting the answers to all five qualification questions before you start pitching your product is that it creates a consultative atmosphere for the buyer/seller relationship. The qualification step is your opportunity to position the needs of the buyer above your own needs.

> The biggest benefit of getting the answers to all five qualification questions before you start pitching your product is that it creates a consultative atmosphere for the buyer/seller relationship.

Restraint on your part is imperative. As sellers, we often have such enthusiasm about our product or service that it's easy to switch the conversation from the buyer and their needs to your perfect solution. You don't want to do that.

Instead, focus on discovering what the buyer needs. If you find out what the person wants and sell them that very thing (assuming that's what you have to sell), then you'll win more often than not. I don't know about you, but I love winning!

8

It's Finally Your Turn to Talk

Full disclosure: This chapter was very difficult for me to write. I have a friend, my book coach Nancy Erickson, who says, "While you're working on your book, your book is working on you." Boy was that true! I kept trying to understand why I was having such a hard time getting this chapter down on paper, and I finally realized that *I don't think I'm all that good at this part of the sales process!*

I sometimes get sidetracked and lost in the details. I get too excited and start talking, and then I literally can't shut up. I bring up product information the client isn't interested in and then confuse the sale altogether. I struggle to think that I'm good at proposals, and I push against the pitch because pitching makes me think of fast-talking slick sales guys in plaid suits.

So in writing this chapter, I wanted to minimize how important it is to be great at proposing a solution that makes your product irresistible. However, I know that a confident, non-arrogant, educational, helpful, caring proposal creates a buying scenario for the customer and sales opportunity for you. I still have so much to learn about elegant proposals. And even though I think connection and qualification trump great presentations, it doesn't mean that proposing, presenting, pitching, or whatever you want to call it, isn't important. It is, and great sales professionals do it at a high level.

You see, the big aha is that *the close really begins during the proposal.* It's critical that you get good at this step. So I'll forge ahead and share what I know about great sales presentations.

The fundamental sales truth I live by is this: find out what the client needs and sell them that. Focus on the buyer, match your product to their greatest needs, and then save something mind-blowing to reveal at the end of your pitch. Temper your enthusiasm so it matches, or is just a notch above, the client's level of enthusiasm so you don't sound over the top with your solution. If what you sell sounds too good to be true, the buyer can become skeptical. Even if it's true, you can break trust with your buyer if you come across as the savior!

Pace Yourself

Before you pitch, make sure you're connected to the buyer and have gone all the way through the qualification process. It's important to me to bring up pacing, because I bet I'm not the only salesperson who gets excited about my stuff and starts running off at the mouth too soon. I've made a ton of mistakes during presentations. I'll find out two or three things I think I need to know from the buyer and rush into pitching my product. If you're reading this book and are in a sales position now, you know what I'm talking about. We want to talk about our stuff. It's almost like we are the championship horse at Churchill Downs, just waiting for the starting gate to open!

The trick is to be patient. Make sure you know everything you need to know before you bust out of the gate with your price or proposal. It can be difficult, if not impossible, to backtrack when you've offered the wrong product or service because you didn't understand the "real" importance of the purchase, or the tolerance for spend, or... remember the five things you must know before you begin your presentation?

Product Knowledge Builds Trust

If you don't know your product, buyers will become suspicious and you will lack confidence. Of course, a sales professional must know their product, but product knowledge alone doesn't set you up to be successful in sales. You must have intimate knowledge of your product—or at the least, a confident way of finding the answers you may not know. I once sold a piece of technology in my sales career. I completely understood how and why the product served the buyer, but I didn't always understand the technology. Luckily, I had a favorite technician I could rely on anytime the buyer asked me something that was over my head!

Never make stuff up. A buyer's "BS meter" is always on high when dealing with salespeople. Unfortunately, the stereotype is a slick talking, plaid suit, sales guy. But if you've followed the Connect-Qualify process, you've already done a lot to build trust. Now is not the time to break that apart. Be confident about the things you know, and confidently help the buyer know that you know how to deal with any unknowns!

Confidence is a funny thing in that it can be difficult to come by until you have the experience of an elegant proposal that works. Here's an example. I once coached a sales gal who was struggling. She was unsure if she was really ready to deliver a confident proposal to a client. She'd been on several sales calls to observe others, and she'd even practiced by role playing with me. However, she was still terribly hesitant to go solo on a sales call. I knew we had to shove her out of the nest, so I asked her what she needed to feel confident. She said, "I need the experience of it going well." In my enthusiasm, I said, "Great! Go deliver the proposal to the client and then you'll have the experience!" I don't know if that was the best advice, but I'm confident that if *experience* is the confidence builder, the more you propose, the better you'll be at proposing. That may seem scary, but it's not rocket science, right? If experience builds confidence, then you better get out there and get the experience! Even the experience of something going wrong will teach you what you don't want to do the next time.

I actually practice what I'm going to say to the prospect—a lot. I rehearse in my head. More than once, I've put pictures and stuffed animals on my desk and practiced giving the presentation to those inanimate objects! I admit the stuffed animals create a bit of a challenge because I prefer to actually have interaction with the customer. The first time Sponge Bob says something back to me, I'll have a heart attack!

Even today, I practice proposals by talking through a presentation with a friend or co-worker before I talk to the client. If experience builds your confidence, and I think it does, then practice. Rehearse your lines with a loved one. Commit to do whatever it takes for you to get comfortable delivering your solution the first time. When you finally do it the first time, you'll build your presentation knowledge, which is more powerful than simply being a product expert. You'll begin to know how the product feels, fits, and serves the buyer. A confident pitch that's focused on the product knowledge as it relates to your specific buyer is a pitch that can win the game every time.

Buyer's Doubt

Presentation time is when all kinds of things start going through the buyer's mind. Until now, there's been a dialogue between the two of you. As a matter of fact, during connection and qualification, you made sure the buyer did the most talking. However, once you get to the proposal stage of the sales process, it's easy for you to slip into a full-blown monologue. Please don't do that. The goal is to keep the buyer engaged in the conversation, continue to build rapport, and to address doubts as they arise.

Doubt may come in the form of an objection and honestly, I hope you get some objections during the presentation because that's the time when you can do something about it. I promise, if you keep the dialogue going

> **If you keep the dialogue going during your pitch, you'll discover any objections that could show up down the road.**

during your pitch, you'll discover any objections that could show up down the road.

Don't talk so much that you lose the attention of your buyer. Their wandering mind may get preoccupied with the price, or they might start worrying about whether they're making the right decision, or if they'll look stupid, or if this solution will work, and on and on. Quell those fears by mingling product education with conversation. Here's how.

Check In with the Buyer

There may be a learning curve when it comes to your product, and this is the time to educate. Much has been written about "educate first, sell second," and I agree—but educating the buyer about your product takes time. It's easy to go on and on about the features and benefits of your stuff. Just be sure to check in with your buyer during this educational phase.

I always want to know how the client is doing throughout the sales process. And I really want to know if they're becoming more or less likely to buy my product. I hate to be told no. Really, I HATE it! The check-in process is what helps me overcome objections before I formally ask them to buy my product or service.

There's a trick I use to keep the buyer involved in the conversation. It's this: *pay attention to your breath.* Whenever you inhale, use that breath as your cue to check in with the buyer. It looks like this...

"Barry, as I've been listening to the challenges you're having with sales growth, it sounds like our sales coaching program might be a great investment. The weekly sales coaching calls and focus on accountability seem to be areas you'd like to improve right away. (Breath) How do you think your team will respond to this type of help?"

This is how I stay focused to propose a solution that matches the buyer's needs, maintain a dialogue with them, and help them insert themselves in the solution I'm proposing.

Concluding the Proposal Part of the Sales Process

During the proposal, it's your time to connect your product to the buyer's desires. A professional proposal isn't a canned, rehearsed, slick sales pitch, nor is it a standard slide deck you use to sell your product. And why not? Well, that slick sales pitch may be the thing that breaks rapport. Sometimes the slick, canned approach trashes the confidence and trust you've built during connection and qualification. The relationship may completely fall apart when you begin to puff up and passionately pitch the powerfulness of your product. After all that puffed-up alliteration, do you see what I mean?

There's a fine line between passion and puffery. I now see the greater impact of my enthusiasm today compared to the over-the-top passion of my younger years. There's a big difference, and I'm not sure I know how to put it in words. Everyone says you must be passionate about your product. But I disagree. I think you must be passionate about what your product *can do*

> Everyone says you must be passionate about your product. But I disagree. I think you must be passionate about what your product *can do for others.*

for others. You must believe in your product, but you can't stop there. People buy what's good for them. They buy because of what they like and want, not what you think is wonderful.

I learned one of my guiding principles in selling from a precious lady named Esther Israel. My first encounter with Esther was at my first Tupperware Rally, where Esther was demonstrating the contents of my new dealer kit. Thank goodness. I desperately needed to know a whole lot more about my products. I was having my first party in two days, and my only product knowledge was how important sippy cups and cereal bowls were for my babies! As a matter of fact, I'd gone to the rally with a goal to exchange the giant Fix 'N Mix Bowl in my kit for Tupper Toys—or anything else I thought I could sell. Boy, was I in for a lesson that has lasted a lifetime!

That night, Esther taught me how to be enthusiastic about what my product could do for others. It was clear that she thought Tupperware was the best product on earth. It lasted a lifetime, and if it ever cracked, broke, chipped, split, or peeled, the company would replace it for free. That, in and of itself, was a great guarantee, and as a buyer you knew that purchasing the product was a good decision. But here's the miracle of a great presentation. Esther stood on the stage with that giant Fix 'N Mix Bowl in her hand, and there I sat, convinced I needed to exchange that very bowl for something else that I could really sell.

Then she helped me see that I could live a better life as the owner of a Fix 'N Mix Bowl. She told me how I could make a big salad just one time during the week and keep it fresh by placing a paper towel over the top, sealing the bowl, burping it, and then storing it upside down in my fridge. The salad would stay crisp and ready for dinner all week long. Making a salad was the most tedious part of preparing dinner, and all I had to do was slice and add a new tomato each evening. I was going to get skinny because of that darned bowl!

And it was also a great popcorn bowl for stay-at-home movie night. Holy cow, I'd get richer by being more frugal about going out to the movies. And by the way, that bowl was big enough to safely bathe a newborn infant. I'd be a better mother all because I owned a Fix 'N Mix Bowl!

That night, I didn't just keep the bowl in my new dealer kit. I bought another one for my own kitchen.

Truly, Esther cared a ton about what Tupperware could do for the people who owned these products, which saved time and money and made food storage and preparation so much easier. I sold Tupperware from 1984 to1995, and I learned so many important sales and life lessons during those eleven years of my life. Loving what you sell, understanding all the features and benefits of your product so you can pull up what you need when you need it, and having fun seem to be critical factors in the buyer/seller relationship.

A Last Word

Depending on what you sell, you might disagree with my presentation beliefs, and that's OK with me. However, I do think that if you focus on the following three things, you'll benefit in two ways. First, you'll provide much more interesting, engaged presentations that are more relevant to the buyer. Second, you'll close more sales more quickly because you found out what the buyer wanted first and then proposed that!

1. Never start a proposal until you have the five things you must learn during qualification.

   a) The why of the buy: what are the hot buttons for the buyer?

   b) The logistics: how many, when are they making the buying decision, nitty gritty stuff

    c) Who's the competition? If they don't buy from you, then who will they buy from?

    d) Are you speaking with the decision maker?

    e) What's the buyer's tolerance for spend?

2. Don't just believe in and have knowledge about your product. Make a commitment to believing in and having a lot of knowledge about what your product or service can do, and has done, for others. Keep the conversation going. Remember, a monologue can alienate the buyer.

3. Pay attention to your breath and check in with the buyer each time you inhale!

9

Late-Term Objections and The Close

C lose the sale. Seal the deal. Consummate the relationship. Get the deposit. Sign the agreement. Call it what you want, but when closing becomes your superpower, you'll go from *surviving* to *thriving*. This is where the rubber meets the road, where you separate the sheep from the goats.

Closing is great fun. Winning the sale is your reward for a job well done. It's what makes all your other work worthwhile. And when you follow the sales process and get the pre-close steps right, closing becomes the natural conclusion.

Don't misunderstand. I'm not suggesting that you can close every opportunity just by becoming proficient at prospecting, connecting, qualifying, and proposing. But I do suggest that it's much easier to ask for the order when you've done those things really well. Plus, you can learn to predict if the client is going to say yes or no, which can help you manage objections before you ask for the order.

The goal is to handle all objections during the qualification stage and to continue to check in and understand the client's position during the proposal. If there are any financial issues, decision maker challenges, competitor issues, or even if you have a sense that what you're selling is not a good fit for the buyer, you'll want to handle those objections before you ask for the buyer's money.

If the deal stalls or dies after the close, recovery can be very painful if not impossible. So before I tell you what a great closer you're going to be, let's address the most common objections.

The Top Five Objections

- I need to talk to someone else.

- The price is too high.

- Not now.

- The dreaded stall

- Silence

The first three objections can be addressed during the qualification process and certainly *should be* addressed before you close.

"I need to talk to someone else."
This objection usually means one of three things:

- I don't know enough to make a decision.

- I can't make the decision because I don't write the check.

- I like you but I don't want to buy your stuff, so I'm going to blame my husband/partner/boss!

So how do you handle this objection? Whenever someone says they need to check with someone else before they buy, I ask, "What do you think they will say?"

This response often prompts the buyer to either list all the reasons why they should buy your product, or they'll reveal a concern that wasn't addressed in an earlier part of the sales process.

It helps you and the buyer gain clarity about what's needed to complete the purchase.

If you have to go back and talk to someone else to close the deal, you're doing twice the work. However, working twice as hard is better than losing the sale because

> So how do you handle this objection? Whenever someone says they need to check with someone else before they buy, I ask, "What do you think they will say?"

you haven't talked to the person who ultimately writes the check. You must become incredibly proficient at understanding who makes the buying decision and connecting directly with them.

The "someone else" objection is usually a nonissue if, during the qualification step, you identify everyone who's involved in making the decision. Remember, this step is one of the five critical things you must learn during the qualification process. So if a question about the decision maker comes up during the closing phase, know that you have room to grow. Retrace your steps to see where you missed identifying the decision makers and make note for the future.

I have to confess that this is my most common mistake. I often connect so well with people that the momentum of building the relationship overrides what I know about the need to identify the buyer. I get excited and make the assumption that I'm talking to the decision maker or that they are the only influencer. So I know plenty about doing double the work. Remember to ask early questions like, "Are you working on this project alone or is someone else helping you?" I would never say, "Are you the decision maker?" because, if they're not, that can alienate this influencer. Instead, I inquire about their role in the company, their focus on the project, and ask what it would mean to them to have an opportunity to work with us. These relationship-building questions will help you discover the ultimate decision maker. In short, do whatever you can to know about the decision makers during qualification.

"Your price is too high; it costs too much; your competitor charges..."

I hate this objection. Hopefully, your product or offering has a value that matches its cost. I used to get defensive and even felt insulted when the buyer didn't want to pay the cost of my product. But now that I have more experience, instead of getting defensive and feeling insulted, I remain confident.

And yet, I don't always get it right. I was recently in final discussions for a big project with people I really liked. My confidence was high, and I felt certain we'd get the deal. But then the most challenging person in the negotiation process spoke up.

"Beth, do you realize how much $53,000 is?"

I assured him that I understood how much it cost to deliver the kind of service we were proposing. I continued, "Just like you, I have to make money in order to continue to help people solve this problem." Oops—wrong approach!

Once I got my foot out of my mouth, I backed up and had a much more respectful conversation. The fact is that making a purchase is a risk, and buyers need to protect their investments. And when there's a financial objection, I think it stems from one of two places:

- Some buyers simply love to negotiate. For some people, negotiating is just part of the game. So I make it simple for them. I ask them what they'd like to take out of the offer so I can lower the price.

   Because there's integrity in our pricing, I stand by my bid. And if the buyer needs a lower price, I offer to sell them less. Don't leave the door open by saying something like, "I'll see what I can do."

   Leave yourself room in the deal in case you're dealing with a negotiator. Know what you can

> Because there's integrity in our pricing, I stand by my bid. And if the buyer needs a lower price, I offer to sell them less.

cut out to lower their cost, and *never, ever sell at your cost!* It's not worth it. I can't think of one time where I flinched on the price and it worked out to be a great deal for me and for the buyer. Not one time!

- Your product isn't a good fit for them. Sometimes the price or the value just isn't right. People value things in their own way. For instance, I'll probably never buy a Tesla. I probably could figure out how to pay for that amazing car, and I'm sure I could be won over by the right sales guy or gal. However, I don't value a car in the same way a Tesla buyer values that type of purchase. On the other hand, I have an extensive art collection that has tremendous value to me, and I probably spent the same amount as I would have spent on a Tesla. I value the artwork, while someone else values a Tesla.

  Here's what works for me:

  a. I enter every sale without making assumptions about what others value. Initially, I don't know the buyer's mind. I have to find out.

  b. I make darn sure I value what I sell. Make sure you do, too. If you don't believe your product is as valuable as the price you charge, then you should consider selling something else.

The "Not Now" and "The Dreaded Stall"

These two objections are closely connected and are usually code for something else you haven't uncovered. I think "not now" has much more potential than the stall, which is usually expressed as some form of "don't call us, we'll call you." In simple terms, we call that a brush-off.

If your prospect tells you that now is not the time to buy, you might ask, "Do you mean *no, not now* or *no, not ever?*" This question keeps the conversation going and allows me to discover the real issue. If they have a real objection, I can usually do something about it, but for me, it's nearly impossible to work against a delay tactic.

It could be that the purchase decision isn't that important to them right now. As a sales professional, it's your job to learn how or why this decision will move to the top of their priority list. You can ask a question like, "How important is it that you make a decision in next thirty days?" Some sales pros may think that question is too pushy, but that type of curiosity-based question helps me learn how to best help the client.

In the case of a "Don't call us; we'll call you," I usually get my feelings hurt! But what actually happened is that I either blew the connection opportunity, or the buyer already has a competitor they prefer, or there's potentially no fit for what I sell or what they're willing to buy. No matter the case, it's tough to be rejected.

At times, you'll win some of the "Don't call us; we'll call you" deals. It's really gratifying when they eventually call. The key is not to give up. If you're interested in this buyer and if they're your ideal client, you may have to remind them many times how your solution can help them. And they may brush you off—that is, until they don't. The salesperson who shows up is the one who wins the most, even when the client has said, "Don't call us; we'll call you."

> The salesperson who shows up is the one who wins the most, even when the client has said, "Don't call us; we'll call you."

Silence

It's hard to interpret silence. And it's uncomfortable. When I verbally ask for an order and the client doesn't respond, I've learned to wait. My impulse is to rush in and fill the silence, but it's wise to wait until they're ready to talk—even two or three seconds can make a difference.

I'm pretty sure my personality style isn't so different from most sales types. We move fast and we process most things out loud. ALERT: There are a whole bunch of other people who process things more slowly, and they do it internally. So sometimes when you encounter silence, it's because the buyer is processing. Give them time. Breathe. If the silence persists, you may lean in, get curious, and ask, "I'm curious to know what you're thinking (or how you are feeling) about the opportunity for us to work together."

In cases where people won't take my phone call or answer an email, I can get very direct. I leave messages or emails that request some type of closure. I might say, "Hey, Bob, this is Beth. I know we worked together on that proposal and I'm taking your silence as a sign we aren't moving forward. Could you please confirm so I can quit bugging you?" I can't tell you how many times that person has immediately picked up the phone and apologized for not getting back to me.

Usually, the priority of the purchase has changed because what was important yesterday became secondary to today's fire. As the sales pro, I have to get in there and remind them why yesterday's stuff still matters.

While late-term objections can be overcome, it's much more difficult at this stage. My primary advice is to make sure you understand and handle all objections before you ask for the order. Once the objections are out of the way, you can get to the very best part of the sales process—the close.

Closing the Sale

Years ago when I wrote a primer about sales, I realized that selling was a lot like dating. I was coaching and training young people at the time and thought they would relate to the dating metaphor.

"When you're dating, you have to prospect, right?" I asked. "At a party you look around and decide who you want to meet.

Next you walk up and attempt to connect. You might even find someone you know in the room to introduce you, which sounds a lot like a referral, doesn't it?"

I asked this group of sixteen- and seventeen-year-olds if they had a favorite line they used when trying to connect. A very enthusiastic young man raised his hand.

"I say, 'I hope your body's name is *Visa* because it's everywhere I want to be!'"

I have to admit, I blushed a bit, but he made my point. His approach was smarmy and funny at the same time, and I'm not sure he got the girl very often. But everyone in the room got his point—that you have to be brave enough to connect first.

The next step is to successfully engage in conversation. The focus is to develop an interesting enough relationship to have a chance for a future date. Those who get real interested in the other person typically have a better shot.

Remember, Alec Grevin, the eight-year-old author of *How to Talk to Girls*, warns against being a show-off. So those who favor "qualification" and ask a lot of questions—like, "What's your favorite food (music, band, etc.)"?—probably fair far better than those who use the "me, me, me" approach. Once you get up enough courage to present the dating option like a movie or a concert, the only thing left to do is to ask this new "prospect" if they'll go out with you. See how the sales process is like dating?

And here's where you may be faced with a problem. Whether you're asking for a date or asking for the sale, the person may say no, which brings up the fear of rejection.

Up until now, everything's gone great. You feel connected, and you might even have a new friend. But then fear takes hold. Crazy things come to mind. In my early sales days, I was such a relationship seller that I'd wimp out and wouldn't ask for the order if I thought there was any chance that buyer would say no.

I want to let you in on two big secrets:

- The fear of rejection is only in your head.

- The customer expects you to ask them to buy your stuff.

Once you get past your fear of rejection, asking for the sale gets easier. When I finally recognized my own inability to close consistently, I became obsessed with learning everything I could about closing the sale. Strengthening this sales skill was a real turning point in my career.

I learned that every single encounter with a prospect should include a close. I prefer to define closing as *having a next step*. I think traditional sales literature would argue that closing is completing the sell, but I disagree. Each opportunity with a buyer includes connection, qualification, proposal, and a close. In my mind, when I've reached my intended objective of a sales meeting, then I've closed. As long as I know what to do next, I feel like I've accomplished the mission.

> I learned that every single encounter with a prospect should include a close. I prefer to define closing as *having a next step.*

Closing could be as simple as setting up the next meeting, finding out who the decision maker is, or even getting a deposit. The larger the price tag, the longer the sales cycle, so closing becomes reaching your intentional closing objective during every sales call.

I once worked with the sweetest young woman in Michigan. Her primary value in life was kindness. As you can imagine, she was a great connector. However, if she said it to me once, she said it one hundred times: "Beth, I just feel so pushy when I press people for the order."

In addition to being a great connector, she was really good at qualifying the prospect, and her proposals were fantastic. As a result, her sales were pretty good. People often said yes during the proposal phase. But she was stuck being a sales amateur. In the interest of not being too pushy, she would never ask the client to buy anything they didn't volunteer to purchase. And that's the difference between being a sales professional and an order taker.

If you've ever been accused of being an order taker, try to improve your closing skills. Even if you are in an order-taking role, you can up your own game by learning to ask for more during the closing phase of the sales process. It's just one more step. You've done all the hard work. Why not get the most out of the order?

Here are two things I did to overcome my own discomfort in asking for the order:

- Disconnect from the outcome.

- In every situation, imagine that everyone says yes every time.

Being disconnected from the outcome takes the pressure off you to sell and off the prospect to buy. It's very comfortable for both buyer and seller. It means that it's OK whether you sell your stuff or not. As the seller, I'm trying to do good things *for* the buyer, not *to* them. And since the buyer doesn't feel any pressure, they're free to make good decisions. When there's no pressure for them to buy anything, it feels like everyone is on the same page.

Assuming everyone will say yes may seem like some type of delusional mind trick, but it works! I love the comfort that comes from imagining everyone wants to buy my stuff. It's a whole lot easier than dealing with the fear they might not. And when people say no, I'm just surprised because I honestly thought they were going to say yes. It never feels like rejection. I simply take it as a lesson and learn something about what it might take to sell to the next person.

Check In with the Buyer

Remember we talked about checking in with the buyer during the proposal phase? In sales language, these are actually called trial closing questions, which are simply key phrases wrapped in curiosity. When you're proposing, remember that every time you breathe, you can use your breath as a cue to stop and check in with the buyer. Sincerely focus on why the buyer believes your product could benefit them.

The following phrases can lead you directly to the close:

"How does that sound so far?"

"How do you think your people will feel about having this service?"

"When you imagine yourself using this product, what stands out to you?"

> When you're proposing, remember that every time you breathe, you can use your breath as a cue to stop and check in with the buyer.

"How do you feel about what you've heard so far?"

Notice that none of these questions is a yes or no question. When you present open-ended questions, it gives the buyer an opportunity to talk. And when the buyer speaks, *listen!* They'll either tell you everything you need to know to finish the deal, or they'll give you a clue about why they aren't yet ready to buy.

When you've finished proposing, it's time to directly ask for the next step if you didn't close the sale during the proposal. I prefer to use an *assumptive close,* and it sounds like this: "Barry, I'm pretty excited about us having the opportunity to work together. I assume you want to get started as soon as possible. All you need to do is sign the agreement, issue a check, and we'll go to work for you as early as next week. What do you think?"

I also like an either-or approach: "Susie, based on everything we talked about, I can fit you in next week or the week after. What works best for you?"

The trick is to find your own comfortable phrases. And then practice asking for the order. Practice out loud. Say only things you sincerely mean.

On the surface, the assumptive sale or the either-or approach may seem manipulative, but they're not. Great selling is about helping others, so it's easy to assume that people want help. It's easy for the buyer to have a choice of either this or that. Both of these direct closing approaches work well as long as you ask for the order or the next step every single time you interact with a prospective buyer.

I'm not afraid of hearing no like I used to be. The truth is that in sales, you get rejected enough times to learn that it won't kill you. Although I am a certified *no* hater, my life, my emotional well-being, and my confidence are no longer tied to whether someone rejects my product or service. It took me a long time to get to this point. I have to admit that at first, it was a bit of a rollercoaster because my worth was linked to how much I could sell. I'm not a psychologist, but I've had enough therapy to realize that whatever you *do* should not define who you *are*.

I have my own bit of superstition when I'm closing a sale. When all else fails, I know I'm about to win the deal when my hands get cold! Sounds crazy I know, but a little crazy goes a long way when it comes to being a sales superstar!

My final words of wisdom about closing come from Nike: **Just Do It!** Ask for the next step in every sales conversation every time.

10

Living the Sales Dream

So can a career in sales really be fun? I think so. My husband is so funny. Every day I head out the door or into my office, he says, "Have fun!" I don't know if it was a trick he was playing on me to make sure I'd contribute financially to the household or if he genuinely thought my work looked like a lot more fun than his. Of course, I was going off to a Tupperware party in my early sales days, and he was an air traffic controller, so I guess there was a difference!

I realize that fun may not be in everyone's DNA. But for me, it's a real core value. Especially in the United States, we spend so much of our time at work. So for me, the sacrifice of time needs to include a fun element.

I love the flexibility of sales. I've spent a lot of my career working from a home office. I really love that option. I know it's not for everyone, but if you have the discipline to manage your own schedule, working from a home office is an incredible opportunity. Research indicates that you can actually save money by working from home. For instance, you have no commute, less need for office clothes, and no need to go out for lunch or buy your coffee. Further, you're more focused. You don't waste time driving, parking, or shooting the breeze with co-workers. All this can add up to as much as $7,000 per year. If you want an instant raise, find a sales position that allows you to work from home. You'll make money before the first sale!

Finally, I find the most joy in meeting new people whom I can help. Remember, great selling is about helping other people. Even in my car sales days (which weren't very fun overall), I had great fun helping a seventy-year-old lady own her first Thunderbird. I have to admit, she looked darn sexy driving out of the dealership parking lot! That was a ton of fun. Today, the hope and delight I see on people's faces when they sign up for our coaching or training services makes it easy for me to invite the next person to do business with us.

Fall in love with the idea of becoming a sales professional!

Own It

Decide today that this is what you want to do. If you're currently in a sales role but aren't experiencing the success you know is possible, then follow the simple sales process steps to move from being a sales amateur to a sales pro. Practice CQPC on a daily basis—with every call. Break the call down and pay attention to where you can improve. I promise, if you will incorporate the CQPC into every conversation, you'll close sales more often and sooner. And don't be afraid to call yourself a sales professional.

Too many times, people in sales roles try to hide the fact they're in sales by using a misleading title. My all-time favorite is *account manager*. Huh? I don't want to manage accounts. Don't get me wrong, I do want to retain accounts, but my business grows when I develop new business. To me, account management sounds like operations. Don't hide what you do with some camouflaged title.

Live It

Do your job on a daily basis—even when you don't feel like it. Maybe *especially* when you don't feel like it. You get to write your own ticket. You don't have to go to the boss and ask for a raise. Just sell more stuff!

Stop depending on someone else to make sure you have enough money. Decide what you want. Do you want to travel? How about a new car? Do you have enough in savings to send your children to college? Can you go out and eat anywhere you want?

The only thing between you and saying yes to every one of these things is your desire and commitment to exercise professional sales efforts. The determination to make one more call to one more prospect, the tenacity to follow the process, and your ability to show up on a daily basis will put you on a path to personal and financial freedom where you can live the life you desire.

Listen, this isn't some overnight success or get-rich-quick scheme. It's a mix of fun and difficulty, joy and disappointment, and most of all, it's within your control.

> **Listen, this isn't some overnight success or get-rich-quick scheme. It's a mix of fun and difficulty, joy and disappointment, and most of all, it's within your control.**

I think it's a pretty big deal when I look around and see so many people who are unhappy with their job. Life is too short to spend so much time wishing you had more money or a better job. Sales gives you a way to live the life you desire.

Learn It

Never, never, never give up. This is a terrific mantra when it comes to sales—and maybe even life. If you're a salesperson who isn't getting what you want out of your career, I know you can do better.

Learn the sales process. Understand that connection with another human is paramount to your success. Build comfort into your relationships as the first step to creating the sale. Just as important, remember to qualify your prospects.

Be interested in others instead of trying to impress them with your stuff. Present your offering in a way that supports everything you learned during the connection and qualification processes.

Remember, it doesn't matter how much you love your product or service. What matters is how much you love what it can do for others, based on what they need or want.

Once you've progressed through the process, you have the right to ask for the business. At this point, people will either buy from you or they won't. As John Maxwell says, "Sometimes you win and sometimes you learn."

I quit being such a no-hater when I realized I could learn a lot more about how to close the next sale if I paid close attention to why I lost the last one. In fact, I once told a non-buyer that I was glad he said no because I didn't understand why everyone else was saying yes! I asked him specifically why he wasn't interested and found out he wasn't the decision maker. I love to learn. It makes me feel like I win every single time!

Love It

Who doesn't love financial and personal freedom? The confidence that comes along with that freedom has made a much bigger difference in my life overall. I love that my career includes human interaction, and because I'm a professional salesperson, I've developed the confidence I need to deal with anyone and everyone.

You have the opportunity to do something big for yourself, your family, your friends, and your future customers. People need each other; we need to interact with each other. We live in an impersonal world, and when you truly connect with others, you stand out. So more than ever, I hope you'll remember that people love to buy things and that when they buy from you, the joy of that interaction is a good thing for them and for you.

People buy from people. And you can be that person!

About the Author

Beth Standlee never met a stranger. A dynamic, enthusiastic liver of life, she dedicates her time to helping others and making their lives better. She is the CEO/founder of TrainerTainment®, a coaching and training enterprise that primarily serves the hospitality industry. Her team provides business coaching, sales coaching, grand-opening strategies, mystery-shopping services, and on-site training.

Beth and her husband, Jerry, are the parents of two adult daughters and an adult son. They live near Fort Worth, Texas.

Please feel free to connect with me on LinkedIn or Facebook or by email at Beth@trainertainment.net